Purls Forever

*The story and legacy of 6 generations of women and
their handcrafted garments*

by Jonelle Raffino

Designed by Big Al Gruswitz

ISBN 13: 978-0-9792017-0-7
ISBN 10: 0-9792017-0-5

Soysilk®, Twizé™, TOFUtsties™, aMAIZing™ are trademarks of the South West Trading Company.

Foreword

by Shannon Okey, knitgrrl.com

Purls Forever *is a loving testament to the legacy every knitter leaves his or her family, and to the bonds that bring them together with or without yarn. As an "accidental knitter" who came into the world of knitting design and publishing without a family tradition as long as Jonelle's, I am in awe. My family is full of painters and artists, but Jonelle's mother, grandmother, great-grandmother—even her great-great-grandmother!— have been creating their own works of fiber art for over 100 years. With this book, you have the opportunity to share in that tradition and create some legacies of your own.*

I've worked with South West Trading Company for a long time—first as a consumer who bought eco-friendly soy spinning fiber from Jonelle, and later as a designer and teacher spreading the word about soy, bamboo and other fibers across the country. From the first moment you meet Jonelle in person, you realize she's a true dynamo, and reading the story of how her company came to life is inspirational no matter what your line of work. Purls Forever *clearly demonstrates that family heritage is not something to be locked away in a box. Jonelle's is alive and well in not only her company, but also the next generation of knitters: her daughters Gianna and Sophia. I hope you will find something to treasure in this book, and that you will be inspired to spread your love of knitting throughout your own circle of family and friends.*

About the Author....

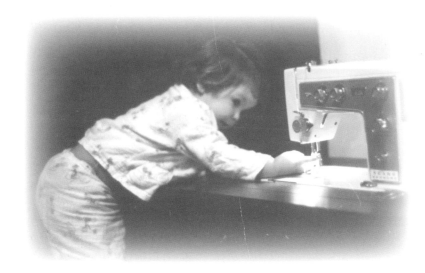

Jonelle Raffino is the creative force behind SWTC INC, the yarn company that brought earth-friendly fibers to the hand knitting industry. A lifelong knitter, crocheter , and fiber artist, Jonelle lives in Gilbert, Arizona with her husband Joe and daughters Gianna and Sophia... and a herd of llamas and angora goats to fuel her fiber addiction.

I've always been fascinated by crafty things. I loved to watch my mother sew and adored the things she made me.

Photo by Fred Neal

My beautiful Family (L-R) Gianna, Jonelle, Sophia, and Joe.

Dedication

Four generations gathered at my christening in 1965. This is me in Nona's arms. On the top left is my mother Jonette and to the right, her mother Josephine.

With this book, I honor the three most influential women in my life: Nona, Nonie, and Mom whose love for each other and for knitting became part of my soul.

Thank you to my father who always encouraged me to write and who bankrolled SWTC for Mom and I—then continued to encourage us and push us when we needed him most. He has been our mentor and our guide.

With love to my husband Joe, who stands beside me and joins me on this adventure. He learned to knit... just to share this journey. It has been wonderful to watch him learn about knitting, yarn, and to champion this business, spearheading our sales. He loves the people in this industry and enjoys being in yarn stores and visiting with knitters. I laugh when I remember him 10 years ago—refusing to follow me in a yarn store and instead opting to stand outside in the cold and read a fishing magazine.

To my daughters Gianna and Sophia. Just hearing them whisper "You can do it Mommy" fueled me in making this dream happen. I find strength in their unwavering confidence in me and hope that someday, they understand that dreams do come true if you work hard, surround yourself with family, and believe that it can happen.

Kat.... You are my rock. I would never forget to mention you. Your copy is autographed!

And most important, to the wonderful owners of boutique yarn stores around the country—I thank you for embracing SWTC yarns and allowing us to learn and grow with you. You have educated us, become our friends, and shared our experiences. We support you with our continued creativity and loyalty.

We encourage you to visit your local yarn store. Many stores also have online capabilities to serve you. A local yarn store will become your best resource in the fiber arts, providing you with personal assistance in planning your project, and guiding you when you have questions. Support them with your loyalty and patronage. They are the foundation of our fiber arts tradition.

All of the yarns in this book are part of the SWTC collection. While I hope you will choose SWTC yarns, which are earth-friendly and spectacularly soft, it is not always possible. Chat with your local yarn merchant, they can help you find the best yarn for your personal taste and budget.

Contents

Patterns

A Common Thread

Marianne Peri, known to all of us as Nona.

*I*n my Italian family, there were two passions that brought us together: good food and good yarn. I remember my great-grandmother, whom I called Nona, knitting constantly. It often seemed like an obsession. In her youth in northern Italy, knitting was necessity. In America, she made wonderful knitted and crocheted garments purely for love.

I remember spending hours at Nona's feet holding my hands in the air. I was a human swift charged with the task of helping wind her yarns into delicate balls. She never wasted a scrap of yarn. Every piece became something. In fact, even old sweaters were subject to remodeling, rewinding, and reworking. What she could create amazed me.

My grandmother, Nona's daughter, was called Nonie. She was also an avid knitter and crocheter. Like most mothers and daughters the bond between them was deep. They would sit together for hours working on their projects, chatting half in English and half in Italian. I loved listening to them. Whenever they started to disagree the conversation got louder until it was completely in Italian. I didn't understand Italian but when two angry women with pointed sticks start to argue, it was always a sight to see. Each had their own distinct design style so they most often clashed over how to accomplish the silliest things. As with everything they were passionate about, every small detail was important, and neither would waiver in their beliefs.

Thanks to Nona and Nonie, every baby born into our family was greeted with a stack of handmade blankets, sweaters, and booties. Each Christmas, we could count on a new sweater and slippers beneath the tree. I have hundreds of crocheted coat hangers that still hang in my closet, and slippers so worn that they hardly cover my toes. I just can't imagine parting with them.

Near my eighth birthday, my family made a trip to a cabin in the snow. This trip is one of my fondest memories.

Nona, Nonie, and my mother sat by the fireplace knitting and crocheting. I curled up on the floor watching needles click and color unfold in their laps. They talked and laughed, bantered back and forth about dropped stitches and how to finish the side of a sweater. Nona never thought anyone's finish work was good enough, which always sparked heated conversation. Every once in a while I would venture closer and hold their balls of yarn in my lap just to be part of their knitting circle. Late that evening Nona asked me if I wanted to learn.

Knitting didn't come easily to me, but I was so proud and determined to learn that I stayed up most of the night practicing.

I was left-handed, which was an oddity in my family. Nona, Nonie, and Mom were all right handed. I sat between them trying to imitate their motions and listen while they all talked at once. I struggled with the simple knit stitches, completely unable to translate it with my left hand. They repositioned my hands, switched my needles and tried tirelessly to help me get it right. We all became frustrated. In the end, I learned to sit across from them and imitate their every move until I was making my first square. I was a knitter.

It was a rite of passage for me. From that day on, I took my place with the women of our family, knitting in their circle. I joined in the conversation, the arguments, and found that with a natural instinct, knitting became a passion. It was our bond. Simple strands of yarn became the thread that tied us together.

Even in her 90s, Nona still spent her days knitting.

When my mother and I opened the old cedar chest, we found it full of handmade treasures from my grandmothers. As each piece was lifted out, my mother recalled who made it, who had worn it, and why. Every piece had a story.

The simple knitted garments had become more than just clothing: they were our family history.

2

The Magic Hope Chest

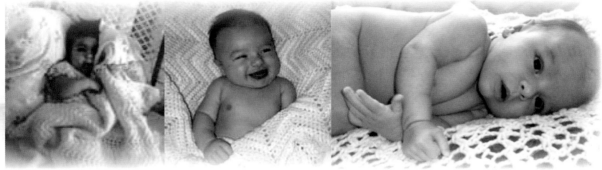

(L-R Jonette, Jonelle, Jonna, and her son, Ethan in blanket from the trunk and from his Nonie, Jonette)

*T*he hope chest became a sad reminder of how much we missed Nonie and Nona when they died. It was packed away one day, holding a history of the happier times and the treasures it would someday pass on to the children of the future.

When my first daughter, Gianna, was born, my Mom dug through the closet to find the old hope chest again. It had been a long time since she had thought of it, but it was time to carry on the tradition and greet a new baby.

In June 2006, my sister had her first child. I had the honor of being with Mom as we opened the hope chest in search of the last of the baby gifts from Nona and Nonie. Much to our surprise, all of Jonna's gifts were knitted in soft greens and yellows, as if they had known we would finally have a boy in our family. Mom added a blanket she had knit in SWTC yarn, telling me that by the time she got her pattern right she could have knit the blanket 6 times, but there wasn't a mistake in it. She was so proud of herself. She added several sweaters and booties, I ceremoniously added the gifts I had made, some from hand-spun wool, some from the yarns I had designed for SWTC. At last we could meet my nephew for the first time.

Arizona Sunset Afghan

Skill level: Beginner ◖☐☐◗

Finished size: 42" wide by 60" long (107 cm by 152 cm)

Gauge: Not important

Materials:

18 skeins SWTC Karaoke (50% Soysilk® fiber/50% wool); color # 300, Dipity

Size H/8/5 mm crochet hook

Yarn needle

Afghan:

Ch 129.

Row 1:

Dc in 6th ch from hook, dc in next 3 chs, *[2 dc in next ch, dc next ch], repeat 5 times, dc next 3 chs, sk2 chs, dc, sk2 chs, dc next 4 chs, repeat from * across to last 3 chs, sk these and dc in last st, ch3, turn.

Row 2:

Work in back loops only from now on.

Ch3 is first dc, sk3 sts, dc next 4 sts, *[2 dc in next st, dc next st] repeat 5 more times, dc next 3 sts, sk3 sts, fpdc, sk3 sts, dc in next 4 sts, repeat from * across to last 3 sts, sk these dc in top of turning ch, ch 3, turn.

Row 3:

Ch3 is first dc, sk3 sts, dc next 4 sts, *[2 dc in next st, dc next st] repeat 5 more times, dc next 3 sts, sk3 sts, bpdc around fpdc of last row, sk3 sts, dc in next 4 sts, repeat from * across to last 3 sts, sk these dc in top of turning ch, ch3, turn.

Repeat rows 2 & 3 until desired length. Finish off and weave ends in.

Please see page 84 for listing of abbreviations.

This beauty is my daughter Sophia. I had to beg for this blanket back and then promise she could have it again later. She loves the bright colors and super soft feel of the yarns.

6

Becoming a Nonie

With the birth of my daughter Gianna, the entire family joined our celebration as we welcomed our beautiful little girl and began our journey as parents. It was a long anticipated and most welcome day for us all. On the day I came home from the hospital with Gianna, my parents were there to greet us. Clutched in my mom's hands were a stack of handmade blankets, sweaters and booties, each with their own story.

Some had greeted me back in 1965, some were made by Nonie and Nona to swaddle the babies they knew we would have and of course, there were beautiful additions my own mother had added to the collection. I had known about these treasures all of my life, but seeing them together with my own baby in my arms was an amazing moment.

I could see my grandmothers in my mind's eye just then. I remembered them more clearly than I had in years, and knew they were with us at that moment. Perhaps the most powerful memory, though, was seeing my own mother hold her first grandchild in a blanket she had knit. It was her rite of passage too. She had become a Nonie.

I remember watching my own Nonie knit a sweater shortly before I left for college. It was a design both ladies had memorized and could knit effortlessly. Nonie told me it was for my hope chest and I laughed out loud, swearing I would never have children! I was off to college then a fabulous career, living the life I dreamed of. I couldn't imagine anything else. Nonie laughed, warning that someday I would have children just like me! My mother said that a lot when she was mad: "You'll understand when you have a daughter JUST LIKE YOU...."

I wasn't a bad kid, but definitely a handful as a teenager, and those curses had an impact, which I'm sure is why I waited so long to have kids. The older I got, the more I worried they really would be like me. I argued with Nonie, saying she was crazy to think I would change my mind about having children... but even then, I secretly knew she was right and looked forward to that time in my life. The little sweater was destined for the old trunk, where it would be safe waiting for me to grow up.

Nona meeting my cousin Michael for the first time with his proud father and my Uncle Jess looking on. Michael has grown into an amazing young man and I know Nona would be proud.

In my mother's arms, I caught a glimpse of the familiar little sweater that my Nonie had made, and it was like seeing an old friend. I was overwhelmed. Even on a sweltering July day in Phoenix, I had to nestle my new baby in it for just a minute. My grandmothers knitted these so that I would remember them and how much they loved me. It was also a message of love for my children from the women who loved them even before they were born.

When Sophia was born 18 months later, my mom was back in action. Her excitement was great fun to witness. Her job was to stay with Gianna while we went to the hospital to have Sophia. This time the hand knit treasures were her own work—signaling the transition from Mom to Nonie had been completed. She had knit for months to ensure that this baby was also greeted with her own pile of heirloom treasures. Much to my surprise, my mother had knit the same little sweater pattern that her mother once made. She had meticulously duplicated it and we now had the pattern forever. Sophia was born on February 1st and as soon as we came home, she was bundled up in a new sweater.

When I pick up my needles, I am inspired by my memories of these great ladies and imagine them channeling generations of knitting wisdom into the yarn. Their knitting was neither complex nor technical. In fact, each piece was notably simple, but reflected an ultimate love of family and lifelong passion for knitting. They will always be the angels of inspiration that sit on our shoulders and guide our hands and hearts for all knitted things. My turn at being Nonie will come way too soon, but I look forward to knitting for my own daughters' hope chests with Nona and Nonie's help.

8

Nona's Baby Jacket with Hood

As designed by and shared in tribute to our Nona, Marianna Peri.

Skill Level: Beginner ◼◻◻◻

Size: One Year

Gauge: 5 stitches = 1 inch (2.54 cm)

8 rows = 1 inch (2.54 cm)

Materials: 4 balls SWTC aMAIZing (100% Corn Fiber) **3 LIGHT**

US size 6 needles (5 mm), or size required for gauge

Yarn needle

Upper Raglan Jacket Section:

Cast on 77 sts. Knit 1 row.

2nd row: K7 (front border), p63, k7.

3rd row: K16 (left front) increase in next st, k1 and mark this st as first "seam" st, increase in next st, k7 (top of sleeve). Increase in next st, k1 and mark it as 2nd seam st, increase in next st, k19 (back), increase in next st, k1 and mark it as 3rd seam st, increase in next st, k7 (top of second sleeve), increase in next st, k1 and mark it as 4th seam st, increase in next st, k16 (right front).

4th row: K7, p71, k7.

5th row: K17, increase in next st, k1, increase in next st, k9, increase in next st, k1, increase in next st, k21, increase in next st, k1, increase in next st, k9, increase in next st, k1, increase in next st, k17.

6th row: K7, p79, k7.

7th row: Work as in 5th row, increase on both sides of the 4 seam sts, having 2 sts more between increases on back and sleeves and 1 at more on fronts.

8th row: Knit all sts; this will form a ridge on right side of work. Continue to work pattern as in these 8 rows, thus in every row on right side increasing in the same 8 places (as in 7th row), and in rows on purled side knitting the first and last 7 sts (for garter stitch front border); every 8th row (wrong side) is always knitted, to form a ridge on right side. When there are 15 increasing rows from beginning, there will be 197 sts on needle and the last row will be the 7th row of pattern. Knit the next row (ridge on right side).

Next row divide for sleeves as follows: k32 sts and slip them to a strand of yarn (left front), knit the next 40 sts and leave them on the needle for the left sleeve; slip the next 53 back sts, the

9

following 40 right sleeve sts and the 32 right front sts—each group to a separate strand of yarn, and tie ends of strands.

Sleeves:

Working from the wrong side on the 40 sleeve sts left on the needle, cast on 4 sts and purl 1 row on all 44 sts; work 5 more rows in stockinette stitch, ending on right side.

Knit next row (pattern ridge on right side). Continue even in pattern for 30 rows; ending on wrong side with 6th row after the last ridge. Next row *k2, k2tog, repeat from * to end (33 sts left).

Knit 8 more rows (4 ridges) in garter stitch; bind off on wrong side, which completes the 5th ridge on right side. Slip the 40 right sleeve sts back to needle; beginning on right side, cast on 4 sts and knit all 44 sts, ending at front edge of sleeve. Continue to work right sleeve to correspond to left. Sew sleeve seams.

Lower Part Of Body:

Beginning at front edge slip the 32 right front sts to the needle, to the same needle slip the 53 back sts; to the other free needle and beginning at left front edge, slip the 32 left front sts. Beginning at left underarm, pick up and k4 sts on the 4 cast on underarm sts, knit the 53 back sts, pick up and k4 sts on the 4 cast on sts at right underarm, knit the 32 right front sts (125 sts on needle). Next row (wrong side) knit the 7 border sts, purl 111 sts, knit the last 7 border sts. Continue in pattern until there are 5 patterns (40 rows) from underarm, ending on wrong side with the 5th ridge. Knit 7 more rows in garter stitch and then bind off on wrong side, which completes the 5th ridge in garter stitch border along lower end of body.

Hood:

Cast on 64 sts. Knit 1 row, purl 1 row, alternately, for 7 rows, ending with a knit row; knit also the next row making a ridge on right side. Repeat these 8 rows, working ridge pattern as on jacket, until there are 40 rows from beginning, ending with the 5th ridge; knit 7 more rows in garter stitch and then bind off on wrong side, which completes the 5th ridge of garter stitch border, same as on lower edge of sweater. Fold hood double and sew edges together at the back.

Finishing:

Sew hood to neck of sweater leaving 4 sts free at each neck edge. Weave in ends.

Please see page 83 for listing of abbreviations.

This is my beautiful sister Jonna and her husband Mark Lewis with their son Ethan.

Time with Nona

During summer vacation of my junior year in college, I returned home. By that time, my grandmother Nonie had passed away from heart problems and my great-grandmother, Nona, was living with my parents. She was in her late nineties, and used to a much slower pace of life. It was hard for her to be at my parents' house—they were always on the go, and everything was strange and unfamiliar to Nona. She tried to find happiness, but she had lived with her daughter for as long as we could remember and the loneliness of outliving not only her but almost all of her friends weighed heavily on her.

I spent a lot of time with Nona that summer and just enjoyed being near her. But I was still a wild college girl! One particular night, my friends and I headed for San Francisco to go night clubbing. It was an awesome evening and we danced until the doors closed behind us. It was 5:00 a.m. when I finally returned to my parents' house. I had planned to sneak into the house and head right to bed. I had the route figured out, avoiding the squeaky floorboard by my parent's room that Dad didn't fix until my sister and I had both moved out for good. Mom and Dad wouldn't be awake for hours.

My plan failed. Nona was sitting at the kitchen table already knitting. I didn't see her—so when she said good morning, I nearly had a heart attack. She laughed so hard she dropped an entire row from her knitting.

She poured me a cup of coffee with so much milk it turned white—just like she had since I was a little kid. Nona called it Italian sweet coffee. She asked where I had been. I stuttered for a minute thinking I could simply say that I fell asleep at a friend's house. Nona seemed to know better, and I could tell I wasn't fooling her. With a quick smile of approval from her, I started to tell her all about my wild night dancing in the city. I described the boys I had danced with, the things I had seen, all of the wonderful music. She listened with a big grin on her face and I just loved sharing all of the interesting details with her. Before long, Nona was telling me all about her younger years—about dating, boys she had met, her wild adventures. She blushed as she recalled her first kiss and giggled like a young girl remembering some of teenage things she did.

It was a side of her I'd never known or even imagined. I realized though, that even generations apart, we were still so much alike.

We talked for hours that morning. She finished the Aran sweater she had been making and I borrowed a set of needles, rummaging through the stash at her side. About 9:00 a.m., my parents rustled into the kitchen. With a wink in my direction, Nona told them I had gotten up early to have coffee and visit and they never knew I had just walked in with the sun. I handed Nona a small coaster I had crafted while we talked, kissed her on the cheek and headed "back to bed".

I still drink my coffee loaded with milk, just as I learned in my childhood... and every now and then, when my daughters wake up early, I pour them a cup of white coffee, sit at the dining room table, and talk with them while I knit.

Felted Karaoke Coaster

Skill level: Beginner ■□□□

Finished size: Approximately 5" before felting and approximately 4" after felting.

Gauge: Not important

Materials: 1 ball SWTC Karaoke (50% Soysilk® fiber/ 50% wool); any color
US size 4 (3.5 mm) double pointed needles
Yarn needle

Coaster: Cast on 6 sts. Knit 1 row.
Increase 1 st in each stitch (12 sts).

Knit 1 row. Increase 1 stitch in each stitch (24 sts).
Knit 4 rows. Increase 1 stitch in each stitch (48 sts).
Knit 4 rows. Increase 1 stitch in each stitch (96 sts).
Knit 2 rows. *Knit 4 sts k2 together. Repeat from * to end.
Knit row.

Bind off and weave ends. When weaving starting thread, use it to close the hole in the center.

Finishing: Felt coaster by tossing it in with your laundry two or three times (hot water with cold rinse recommended). Do not use bleach, or detergent with bleach. Karaoke produces a beautiful, soft felt.

A Dress for Josephine

"*T*hat was your Nonie's dress" my mother sighed. "I kept it because it reminded me so much of her. She looked so beautiful in it." We called my grandmother Nonie, but to the rest of the world, she was Josephine Marie Peri.

Nonie was a beautiful lady who never fully understood how wonderful and how pretty she really was. Born in San Francisco in 1920, she was the first generation of our family born in the USA. Both of her parents came from Italy, finally making a home in Napa, California.

Josephine Marie Peri, was my grandmother who I knew simply as Nonie.

Like her mother, Josephine was a simple woman who identified herself closely with Italian culture. Her Italian was more fluent than her native English. She married young, had 2 children, divorced, and remarried a wonderful man later in life. She was dedicated to her family and stayed near her mother her entire life. They had a very special bond.

Even if she had money to spend, Nonie rarely spent it on herself. Most of her finest things were knit or crocheted, some hand sewn. Her mother made clothes for her with the finest yarns they could afford, allowing her to have fashionable garments despite the budget constraints of her family.

Hand-knit by her mother, my Nona, this elegant skirt and top set were made for Josephine to wear to a special party when she was in her 20s. It sported an A-line shape with a picot stitch pattern throughout. The interesting finish of the waistline allowed the elastic to be adjusted easily. My own mother adored this sweater and skirt, and after Nonie passed away she tucked it in her own dresser for safekeeping. From time to time she, too, wore it to a party or special evening out. It made her feel connected to her mother, which she said gave her confidence whenever she needed it most.

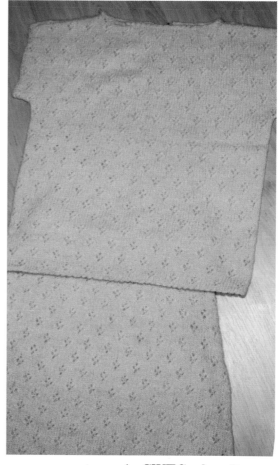

The women in our family have always been close. Nonie and Nona lived together or at least very close by each other most of their lives. My mother talked to her mom daily. In fact, we always knew when she didn't, as an argument would ensue the next day. Nonie could be a bit dramatic about how worried she was when her daughter didn't call. I suspect it's a genetic thing— my mom checks on us daily, too. Luckily, I have e-mail, which makes it a bit easier for us both... and since we are partners in SWTC, she sits about 10 feet from me Monday through Friday.

Time has begun to break down the yarn, which has become brittle and weak, but the garment was and is still exquisite and timeless.

14

Bamboo Eyelet Set

A classic skirt and top set never goes out of style. The picot edging of the top is repeated at the skirt's hem. And bamboo fiber makes it very pack-able for a trip.

Skill Level: Intermediate ◼◼◼◻

Size:

Woman's small (medium, large, extra-large) Instructions are given for smallest size, with larger sizes in parentheses. When only 1 number is given, it applies to all sizes. Model shown in size small.

Finished Measurements:

Chest: 35 (37.5, 42, 46)"/89 (95, 107, 117) cm

Waist: 28 (30, 32, 34)"/71 (76, 81, 86) cm

Hips: 39 (41, 43, 45)"/99 (104, 109, 114) cm

Skirt length: 26" (66 cm)

Skirt width at hem: 45 (47, 49, 51)"/(114, 119, 124, 130) cm

Materials:

SWTC Bamboo (100% Bamboo);
(100 g/250 yds per ball): #521 Chocolate 🧶 **3** LIGHT

Top: 3 (4, 4, 5) balls
Skirt: 4 (4, 5, 6) balls

US size 4 (3.5 mm) 24" circular needles, or size required for gauge

US size 5 (3.75 mm) 24" circular needles, or size required for gauge

Size F/5 crochet hook

Stitch markers in 3 different colors

1 yd (1" [2.54 cm] wide) elastic

Coordinating color sewing thread

Gauge:

22 sts and 30 rows = 4" (10 cm) in eyelet pattern with larger needles

23 sts and 32 rows = 4" (10 cm) in stockinette with larger needles

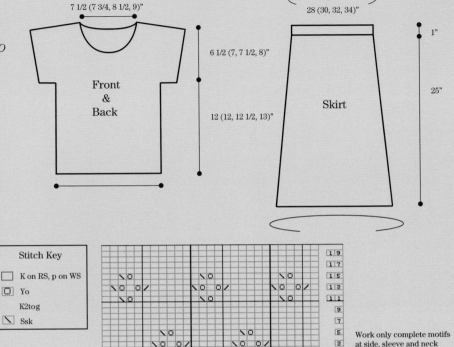

Stitch Key
- ☐ K on RS, p on WS
- ⊡ Yo
- K2tog
- ◩ Ssk

Work only complete motifs at side, sleeve and neck edges.

Notes:

Top is worked back and forth in two separate pieces. Work only complete motifs at side, arm, and neck edges. If there are not enough stitches to complete a motif, work them in stockinette. Skirt is worked in the round from waist down on circular needles.

TOP

Back:

With larger needles, cast on 97 (103, 115, 127) sts. Purl 1 row, knit 1 row, purl 1 row.

Picot Turning Row (RS): K1, *YO, k2tog; rep from * across row. Purl 1 row, knit 1 row, purl 1 row.

Joining Row (RS): Fold hem with WS tog. *Insert RH needle into next st, then into cast-on st and K2tog; rep from * across row. Purl 1 row. Set up pattern (RS): Beg at chosen size on chart, work to A, rep between red lines to last 11 (9, 10, 11) sts, work from B to end of chart.

Work even in established pat until back measures 12 (12, 12.5, 13)" from beg, ending with a WS row.

Please see page 83 for listing of abbreviations.

Begin sleeves:

Cable cast on 11 sts at beg of next 2 rows. Inc 1 st each end every 8th (8th, 8th, 10th) row 6 times - 131 (137, 149, 161) sts.

Work even until armhole measures 6.5 (7, 7.5, 8)" above cast-on sleeve sts, ending with a WS row.

Shape back neck and shoulders:

Mark center 35 (37, 41, 45) sts.

Next Row (RS): Work to first marker, join second ball of yarn and bind off marked sts, remove markers, work to end of row.

Working on both sides of neck with separate balls of yarn, dec 1 st at each neck edge every row 3 times, at the same time bind off at each arm edge 12 (11, 12, 13) sts once, then 11 (12, 13, 14) sts 3 times.

Front:

Work as for back until front measures 2.5 (3, 3.5, 4)" above cast on sleeve sts, ending with a WS row.

Shape front neck:

Mark center 31 (33, 37, 41) sts.

Next Row (RS): Work to first marker, join second ball of yarn and bind off marked sts, remove markers, work to end of row

Bind off at each neck edge 2 sts twice, then 3 sts once.

Continue with incs at arm edge while working neck edge even until sleeve measures same as for back above cast-on sleeve sts.

Shape shoulders:

Bind off at each arm edge 12 (11, 12, 13) sts once, then 11 (12, 13, 14) sts 3 times.

Finishing:

Sew shoulder, sleeve and side seams.

Crochet Neck Edging:

Beg at seam, work 1 row sc around neck edge making sure to keep work flat.

Join with sl st.

Rnd 2: Working from left to right, work 1 sc in each sc of previous row. Join with sl st and fasten off.

Rep edging around lower sleeve edges.

SKIRT

Beg at waist with smaller needles, cast on 162 (174, 186, 198) sts.

Beg with a purl row, work in stockinette for 9 rows.

Turning Row (RS): Purl. Join without twisting, pm between first and last st.

Change to larger needles and work in rnds from this point.

Knit 9 rnds.

Join for casing.

Fold waistband to inside. With WS tog, *insert RH needle into next st, then into cast-on st and k2tog; rep from * around.

Place markers after every 27 (29, 31, 33) sts in following color sequence: A, A, B (left seam), C, C, end of rnd (right seam) marker. Markers between side seams denote placement of front and back darts.

*Knit 7 rnds.

Inc Rnd: [Knit to st before marker, work R inc, knit to next marker, sl marker, work L inc, knit to seam marker, work Dbl inc] twice.*

Rep from * to * 7 times more - 226 (238, 250, 262) sts.

Remove dart markers, leaving only end of row and left seam markers.

**Knit 7 rnds.

Inc Rnd: Work Dbl inc at each marker as established.**

Rep from ** to ** 7 times more - 258 (270, 282, 294) sts.

Remove left seam marker and work even until skirt measures 26" or desired length above waist turning rnd.

Picot Turning Rnd: *YO, k2tog; rep from * around.

Knit 8 rnds. Bind off loosely.

Finishing:

Cut elastic 1" longer than desired waist measurement. Thread elastic through waist casing. Overlap ends by 1" and sew securely. Sew waistband opening at right seam.

Turn hem to inside and stitch in place.

Gianna's First Birthday Dress

My oldest daughter Gianna just celebrated her 7th birthday. Her room is skillfully decorated in shades of pink and lilac with a princess theme. It's her castle—full of teddy bears collected from her first days nestled among all of her treasures, creations, and possessions.

On a recent expedition into her room, a small white teddy bear captured my attention and brought me back to a moment I treasure. The Bear's little pink dress was made by my mother as a gift to Gianna, her first grandchild. I hadn't seen this dress in years.

Knit from lightweight cotton, the dress challenged Mom from start to finish, but was one of her favorite gifts ever given. The day of Gianna's first birthday, my mother showed up unusually early. I later found them together in Gianna's room. Mom was sliding the little pink dress over Gianna's head, explaining that she had made it all herself. My mother was choked up with pride.

Gianna stood quietly playing with the tie on the dress—tasting it, musing over it and watching her grandma talk. I could feel the tears well up in my eyes as I listened to my Mom shared the story of this knitted dress and how it came to be. She described her quest for the perfect yarn, the challenge of the lost stitches, and how much it meant for her to make this for her first grandchild.

Gianna may not remember that day, but I will never forget it.

aMAIZing™ Little Pink Dress

The little dress was knit from a pattern Mom found using a cotton yarn. Once stained, it has never become clean again. We redesigned our own version using aMAIZing™, the SWTC yarn made from corn fiber. It's machine washable and dryable, which we think is a better choice for child's dress.

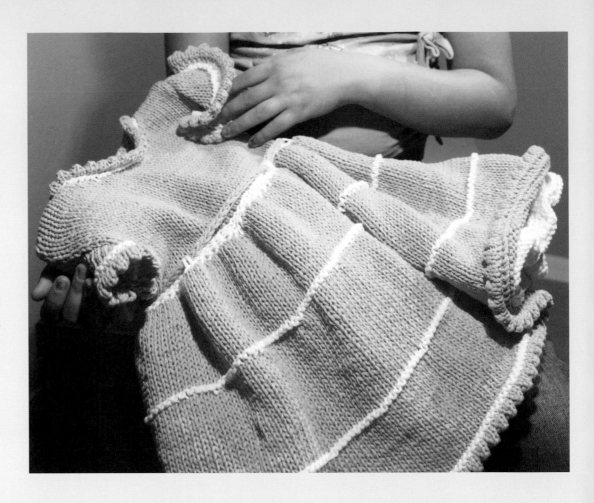

Skill level: Intermediate ◼◼◼▭

Sizes:

Chest: 20"/22" (50/56 cm)

Length: 17"/19" (43/48 cm)

Gauge:

18 sts= 4" (10 cm) in St st

Materials:

SWTC aMAIZing (100% Corn Fiber)

MC = 5, 6 balls (pink)

CC = 4, 5 balls (white)

US size 5 (3.75 mm) & 8 (5 mm) 24" (61 cm) circular needles, or sizes required for gauge

Stitch marker

3 stitch holders

This dress is worked starting with the skirt and working from the waist down. The bodice is worked from the waist up.

Skirt:

Using CC and smaller needles, cast on 80/90 sts and knit 6 rows. Cut CC and with MC and larger needles (k1, m1) repeat to end of row, 160/180 sts. Purl 1 round.

Work in St st for 1.5" (3.75 cm). Join and work in the round in stst (knit all rows) placing marker at the join. When the MC section measures 3"/3.5" (7.5/9 cm), CC (k8/9, M1) repeat around, (178/199 sts).

With CC, knit 1 round, purl 1 round. With MC, knit for 3"/3.5" (7.5 /9 cm). With CC (k8/9, M1) repeat around ending with knit to marker. (204/220 sts) purl 1 round. With MC, knit for 3"/3.5" (7.5/9 cm).

With CC, knit 1 round, purl 1 round. With MC, knit 2 rounds. (YO, k2tog) repeat around. Knit 2 rounds.

The bind off round is easier to work with when the purl side is facing you. Pick up the purl st 5 rows below and purl tog with the next st on the left needle. Repeat this step and pass the first over the last st and off the needle.

Continue to purl and then bind off around. Weave in all ends.

Please see page 83 for listing of abbreviations.

Bodice:

With larger needles, purl 80/90 sts along the top of the waist band. Cast on 1 st, k1, purl to end. Cast on 4 sts and knit to end.

1. K1, p80/90, k4.

2. Purl.

3. K2, YO, k2tog, knit to end (button hole).

4. Purl.

Repeat rows 1 & 2 for 1.25"/1.5" (3.5/3.75 cm), then repeat rows 3 & 4.

Continue in pattern for 2.5"/3" (6.25 /7.5 cm), for 20" (50 cm) size, k25, turn and finish the right back.

For the 22" (55 cm) size, k28, k2tog, turn and finish the right back. Right back, continue in St st for 3"/3.5" (7.5/9 cm) remembering to work buttonholes as you go. Bind off all but 10 sts at the shoulder edge.

Rejoin yarn and k40/44, turn and work in stst for 1.5"/2" (3.75/5 cm). K16/17, place next 8/10 sts on a holder, turn and bind off 4 sts and p to end. Knit 1 row, turn and bind off 2 sts and purl to end. Knit to last 3 sts, k2tog, k1. Repeat this last row until there are 10 sts remaining, place those 10 sts on a holder.

Rejoin yarn for the right shoulder and bind off 4 sts, knit to end. Purl 1 row, bind off 2 sts and knit to end. Purl 1 row. k1, ssk, knit to end. Purl.

Repeat these last 2 rows until there are 10 sts remaining and place these sts on a holder.

Rejoin yarn to the remaining 20/22 sts for back and work in St st knitting the 1st st on the purl side each time until it measures the same as the other back. Bind off on a purl side row, leaving the last 10 sts.

Knit together bind off: with right sides facing and a 3rd needle, knit 1 front st & 1 back st tog, repeat bind off the shoulder sts.

Neck trim:

With right side facing, pick up 4 sts on top of the buttonhole band, 12 sts to the shoulder seam, 12 sts down front slope, 8/10 sts from holder, 12 sts up shoulder slope and 12 sts along back. Purl 1 row, knit 1 row, purl 1 row. K1, (YO, k2tog) repeat ending with k1, purl 1 row, knit 1 row, purl 1 row. Cut the yarn

leaving about a yard and with a tapestry needle, sew each st down to the pick up row sts. Do not pull tight enough to pucker. Fasten off yarn and weave in all ends.

Sleeves: (make 2)

Using larger needles and waste yarn (contrasting color yarn to be cut away later), cast on 70 sts. With MC, work St st for 4 rows. K1, (YO, k2tog) repeat ending with k1. Beginning with a purl row, St st for 4 rows ending by working a knit row. Pick up 1 st on the first row and purl it together with the first st on the left needle. Continue until all 1st row sts have been purled together with all the last row sts. Remove the waste yarn. K2tog along next row. Purl 1 row. With CC, knit 2 rows. With MC knit 1 row, purl 1 row. Bind off 3 sts at the beginning of every row until there are no sts left.

Petticoat:

Turn the dress inside out. Using smaller needles and CC, on the last waistband row (just at the top of the skirt) pick up 80/90 sts. Beginning with a purl row (the purl side of the skirt and the knit side of the petticoat should be facing each other), increase in each st. (160/180 sts.) Work St st for 1.5" (3.75 cm). Join and work in the round for 6"/8". Increase in each st around, 320/360 sts total. (K9, sl1) repeat to end of round. Repeat this round 3 more times. (YO, p2tog, p5, p2tog, YO, k1) repeat to end of round. Repeat these 4 rows 3 times. Bind off loosely.

Finishing:

Weave in all ends. Sew on buttons. Sew in the sleeves.

I-cord ribbon:

Cast on 3 sts, k3, slide sts to the other end of the needle and k3. Continue for 40" (101 cm), k3tog and fasten off. With CC, sew belt loops 1" (2.5 cm) in from each end of waist band and every 3" (7.5 cm) around.

Sophia's New Blanket

Nona made this blanket for me and wrapped me in it when I was born. She knit and crocheted until she died of a stroke just shy of her 99th birthday. Nona was a simple knitter using whatever yarns she could afford or salvage from an aging sweater. She mixed color with simple techniques and never wrote a single pattern down. She would just knit. As the family matriarch, she made it her duty to teach every girl how to knit.

I found my youngest daughter Sophia curled up in this old blanket on the couch one morning. I didn't know where she had found it, but like seeing an old friend, the mere sight of the brightly colored and slightly worn-out blanket brought tears to my eyes. I sat quietly on the floor next to Sophia absorbing the moment, remembering my great-grandmother and this wonderful gift that would now be handed from mother to daughter.

This blanket was the first given to me just shortly after I was born, hand crocheted by Nona. It was my safety as an infant, my shelter as a child, and one of my most treasured possessions as an adult. The blanket and I are over 40 now and both show signs of gentle wear and tear.

As Sophia woke up, she noticed me sitting quietly next to her, holding the edge of the blanket. A tear rolled from my eye when she asked me if I was mad that she had taken the blanket from my trunk. I smiled and then found the words. "It's what Nona would have wanted, Sophia. It's yours now."

Blanket Redux

Simple double crochet shells knit in long vertical rows with scraps of yarn from her stash make this blanket colorful and fun. The shell border finishes it. The pattern has been updated a bit using Karaoke from SWTC, and we gave it a wonderful Southwestern flavor to reflect our Arizona home. Karaoke is 50% Soysilk®/50% wool.

Skill level: Beginner ■□□□

Finished size: 44" wide by 56" long (112 by 142 cm)

Gauge:

4 shells = 4" (10 cm)

7 rows = 4" (10 cm)

Materials:

SWTC Karaoke (50% Soysilk® fiber/50% wool); (4) MEDIUM
(50 gm, 100 m)

Size G/6/4 mm crochet hook

Yarn needle

Notes:

Pattern can be made any size by using a multiple of 4.

Change colors as desired at end of row.

Blanket:

Row 1:

Ch172, work shell st in 4th ch from hook, * sk3 chs, work shell st, repeat from * across, dc in last st, ch3, turn.

Rows 2 - 112:

* Shell in ch1 sp, repeat from * across, dc in last st, ch3, turn.

Border:

Row 1:

Work sc evenly around afghan.

Row 2:

*Sl, sc, hdc, dc, trc, dc, hdc, sc; rep from * around.

Please see page 84 for listing of abbreviations.

To Break the Curse of the Boyfriend Sweater...

Marry Him.

This is my wonderful husband Joe, proudly wearing his sweater.
I'm really glad the curse is gone... he wants another one.

*E*very knitter has heard about the curse of the boyfriend sweater. I am a believer—it's not just urban legend.

After 6 months of dating, I knit my first serious boyfriend a sweater. I labored over it, knitting in every spare minute. It was my freshman year in high school. Of course, knitting wasn't in vogue then, so I couldn't risk being seen with yarn in my bag. This meant I spent a lot of extra time at home to make this labor of love.

The sweater was a cabled pullover in the best yarn I could afford and I proudly presented it to him after a school dance. I could tell by the look on his face that this wasn't a good idea. He could tell by the look on my face that he had better wear it! I took his lackluster thank you pretty hard and the relationship dwindled fast. It would be college before I challenged the curse again… and became a believer for life.

By my 31st birthday I met the man I would marry. A year into our courtship, he asked me if I would knit him a sweater. That day is still clear in my memory. I felt my heart pound, my hands sweat. A loud voice in my head yelled, "ARE YOU BREAKING UP WITH ME?" I remained quiet, shrugging my shoulders and finally whispering, "Someday."

I eventually bought some yarn and half-heartedly showed him a picture of what I could make. After our second year of dating I finally cast on. I remember one day I was particularly mad at him. I raced to the boyfriend sweater and knit for hours, convinced that I would teach him a lesson—I just had to finish it! Luckily, I cooled down. Joe and I were married in 1999.

I finished that sweater and gave it to him after our first anniversary. We had a great laugh as I told him how I had broken the curse of the boyfriend sweater—or at least eluded it. He laughed when he realized the sweater would no longer fit!

I redesigned it here. The original sweater reflected his New Jersey upbringing. It was a heavy winter sweater in the warmest wool you could imagine. Jersey Joe, as I've always called him, now makes Arizona home. It's hot here most of the year and casual all of the time. So here is Joe's boyfriend sweater with a lighter yarn and a southwestern flair. I think the curse of the boyfriend sweater is just another version of the Snow White story. Once you have found true love, the curse disappears.

Boyfriend Sweater in Pure

Skill Level: Intermediate ◼◼◼◻

Finished Chest Sizes: 42 (46, 50, 54, 58)"

Gauge: 24 sts and 32 rows = 4" in pattern stitch on larger needles

Materials:

SWTC Pure (100% Soysilk® fiber) [3 LIGHT]

MC = Sapphire 9 (14, 14, 19, 24) skeins

CC = Parrot 4 (4, 4, 6, 6) skeins

US size 3 (3.25 mm) & 5 (3.75 mm) straight needles, size 3 (3.25 mm) circular 24" (61 cm) for neck edging, or sizes required for gauge

Stitches used:

1 x 1 rib (multiple of 2 + 1)

RS rows: Knit 1, *p1, k1; repeat from * across.

WS rows: Purl 1, *p1, k1; repeat from * across.

7 x 1 rib (multiple of 8 + 1)

RS rows: Knit 1, *k3, p1, k4; repeat from * across.

WS rows Purl 1, *p3, k1, p4; repeat from * across

Notes:

Back is 2" (5 cm) longer than front. Side slits continue 3" (7.5 cm) up from hem. Sleeves are picked up from body & knit downward. Body & sleeves are worked alternating 2 rows MC & 2 rows CC in 7 x 1 rib.

Sweater:

Back:

With MC and smaller needles, cast on 129 (137, 153, 161, 177) sts. Work in 1 x 1 ribbing for .75", ending after a WS row. Change to larger needles and CC. Keep 1 x 1 rib over first 8 sts, then 7 x 1 rib across row to last 8 sts, keep 1 x 1 rib on last 8 sts. Work next row in established pattern in CC. Continue in set patterns working 2 rows MC and 2 rows CC throughout until back measures 4" from beg. Ribbed edges for side slits are complete. Now work all sts in 7 x 1 rib and 2 rows of each color. Continue to work even until back measures 28 (30, 31, 33, 34)" from beg. Place 40 (44, 62, 66, 74) sts at each end on holders for shoulders and center 49 sts on holder for back neck.

Front:

Work same as for back until front measures about 2" from beg, ending side vent ribbing with same color stripe as back. Change to 7 x 1 rib & work until front measures 19 (21, 22, 24, 25)". Divide for neck placket: Next RS row, work across 60 (64, 72, 76, 84) sts & place on holder. Work right front: Work 1 x 1 across next 9 sts & continue 7 x 1 rib across row. Work even, keeping 9 sts at center edge in 1 x 1 ribbing & remainder in 7 x 1 rib until front measures 23 (25, 26, 28, 29)" from beg. At neck edge, bind off 19 sts, then dec 1 st at neck edge every RS row 10 times. Continue even on 40 (44, 62, 66, 74) sts until front measures same as back to shoulder. Place all sts on holder for shoulder.

Left front:

Replace sts to needle, ready to begin a WS row. Cast on 9 sts for placket (or pick up 9 sts from right front placket). Keep center edge 9 sts in 1 x 1 rib & remainder in 7 x 1 rib same as for right front, and AT THE SAME TIME work buttonholes. When placket measures 1" & 3" (2.5/7.5 cm), make button hole on RS by working k1, p1, YO, k2tog, p1, k1, p1, k1. Continue left front shaping same as for right front.

Shoulders:

Join shoulders using 3 needle bind off. Holding front and back right sides together, work 3 needle bind off: Put right needle through 1st stitch on front needle then through 1st stitch on back needle, knit as usual. Repeat for 2nd stitch. Two stitches now are on right needle. Lift right-most stitch over last stitch knit and off the needle. One stitch now bound off. Repeat across each shoulder. Measure down from shoulder seam 10 (11, 11, 12, 12)" on front and back for sleeve placement.

Sleeves:

With MC, pick up 121 (129, 129, 145, 145) sts between markers. Working 7 x 1 rib & 2 rows per color, dec 1 st each edge every 4th row 12 (13, 13, 11, 11) times, then every RS row 0 (0, 0, 7, 7) times. 97 (103, 103, 109, 109) sts. Work even until sleeve measures 8" from shoulder. If sleeve length is shortened, decreases will need to be worked more often. Change to smaller needles & MC. Work 1 x 1 ribbing .75" (2 cm). Bind off sts.

Please see page 83 for listing of abbreviations.

Collar:

With circular needle and MC, pick up and knit approximately 26 sts from WRONG SIDE of right front edge, purl 49 sts from back neck holder and pick up 26 sts from WS of left front edge. Do not pick up sts from 9 st placket at front edges. When collar is folded down, the inside shows more than the outside, so picking up from the WS gives a neater and smoother neck edge. Work collar in 1 x 1 ribbing for 3" (7.5 cm) or desired length. Bind off all sts.

Determine pocket placement by measuring and marking center of left front between placket and sleeve edge. Bottom of pocket should be about 2" (5 cm) below sleeve placement. Run a 8" (20 cm) length of contrasting yarn through stitches for lower edge of pocket

Pocket:

Fold front WS together along pocket placement row. With smaller needles and MC, pick up 25 sts from left front for pocket. Change to larger needles and work in stockinette until pocket measures 3.25" (8.25 cm) from beg. Change to smaller needles and work in 1 x 1 ribbing for .75" (2 cm). Bind off all sts. Sew sides of pocket in place to body.

Finishing:

Sew buttons under buttonholes on right front.

A Sweater
for Dad

*F*inding this yoke sweater in the old trunk had us all laughing. It was loosely based on a Nordic sweater pattern I had found, but I incorporated my precious hand-spun yarn, and modified the design to make it more simple.

I made this sweater shortly after I had learned to spin. I was living in Chicago at the time, and found an arts center near Lincoln Park where I lived. I would walk proudly to class, carrying my rented spinning wheel each week. I remember falling flat on my back in the snow one day—I somehow managed to hoist the wheel over my head and into the air. I had a knot on my head, a giant bruise, and hobbled in to class too sore to spin... but the wheel was unharmed.

The yarn in this sweater was terribly uneven and over-twisted in places, but I was so proud of it all. The multi color yoke allowed me to hide some of the flaws and use up a lot of the small skeins I had made while experimenting and learning. My parents were stationed in Boston during the winter of this particular year. They were working in telecommunications, building tower sites. The weather was harsh like Chicago and Dad constantly complained about how cold he was. This sweater was for him. I worked on it non-stop to have it ready in time for Christmas. I spun 8 different yarns for the yoke and selected exquisite commercial wool to match. I knit in every spare minute.

We all met in Napa for the holidays. We are a small family, but the holidays always bring us home. I spent Christmas Eve sleeping in the airport. Chicago O'Hare shuts down frequently due to weather, particularly in the winter. I knew it was a risk at the holidays, but I was determined to be with my family. Christmas day, I was fortunate enough to get on the first flight and arrived in San Francisco before noon—then on to Napa in time for Christmas dinner. I was exhausted and disheveled... but home.

We have always exchanged gifts on Christmas Eve, leaving Christmas day to Santa Claus. This time, the family waited until I could join them. I shared the gifts I had brought and opened all of the wonderful things for me. For Mom, I brought 6 big skeins of yarn I had made myself.

I saved Dad's sweater for last. I could tell he loved it—or the thought of it. He put it on so everyone could see the beautiful job I had done. I told the family about my spinning lessons, the wheel I was buying and how hard I had worked to get the sweater done in time. As I chattered on, Dad began to scratch his neck, itch his arms, and look genuinely uncomfortable. I had never seen him in a wool sweater and now I realized why. It itched. I suggested he wear a shirt under it and with an uncomfortable smile, he agreed.

A week after Christmas, I got a call from Mom and Dad. They had been transferred from the project in Boston to a long-term contract in Los Angeles. Now they would be able to spend more time at their house in Phoenix too.

The Nordic sweater hadn't even made it to Boston, and would never be needed in Los Angeles (where a cold day hovers in the 60s). It was really fun to see him put the sweater on to get a picture for the book. Even this many years later, it was a proud moment.

Karaoke Yoked Cardigan

Skill Level: Intermediate ◼◼◼◻

Size: Adult small (medium, large, extra-large, 2X-large) Instructions are given for smallest size, with larger sizes in parentheses. When only 1 number is given, it applies to all sizes. Model shown in size medium.

Finished Measurements:

Chest: 36 (40, 44, 48, 52)"/91 (101, 112, 123, 132 cm)

Side to underarm:
13 (14, 15, 16, 16)"/33 (35.5, 38, 40.5, 40.5 cm)

Yoke depth: 8 (8.5, 9, 9.5, 10)"/20 (21.5, 23, 24, 25.25 cm)

Sleeve length:
17.5 (18, 19, 20, 20)"/44.25 (45.75, 48, 50, 50 cm)

Materials:

SWTC Karaoke (50% Soysilk® fiber/50% wool); 8 (9, 10, 12) balls #295 Black; 3 (4, 4, 5) balls #306 Epiphany

US size 5 (3.75 mm) 16" (40.5 cm) and 29" (73.5 cm) circular needles

US size 6 (4mm) 29" (73.5 cm) and 36" (91.25) circular needles, or size required for gauge

Stitch markers and holders

Separating zipper

Gauge:

19 sts and 26 rows = 4"/10 cm in stockinette

Notes:

Circular needle is used to accommodate large number of sts. Do not join; work in rows.

Work sleeves first and use them as your gauge swatch.

W&T (Wrap & Turn): Bring yarn to front of work, sl next st to RH needle purlwise, take yarn to back of work, replace st to LH needle, turn.

1/1 Ribbing

Row 1 (RS): K1, *p1, k1; rep from * across.

Row 2: P1, *k1, p1; rep from * across.

Rep Rows 1-2 for pat.

33

Cardigan

Sleeves:

With MC and smaller needles, cast on 33 (39, 43, 47, 55) sts. Beg with a WS row, work even in 1/1 Rib for 2.5" (6 cm), inc 6 (6, 6, 6, 8) sts evenly on last WS row - 39 (45, 49, 53, 63) sts.

Change to larger needles. Working in stockinette, inc 1 st each end every 8th row 11 (12, 12, 14, 15) times - 61 (69, 73, 81, 93) sts.

Work even until sleeve measures 17 (17 1/2, 18 1/2, 19 1/2, 19 1/2)" from beg, ending with a WS row.

Join CC. Referring to chart, work 4 rows in color pat, cutting MC after row 3 and working with CC only from this point.

Bind off 7 (8, 10, 11, 12) sts at beg of next 2 rows. Place rem 47 (53, 53, 59, 69) sts on holder.

Body:

With MC and smaller needles, cast on 153 (171, 189, 207, 223) sts.

Next row (WS): Sl1, *k1, p1; rep from * across.

Slipping first st of every row, work even in 1/1 Rib for 2" (5 cm), inc 16 (18, 20, 22, 24) sts evenly on last WS row - 169 (189, 209, 229, 249) sts.

Change to larger needles. Keeping 6 sts at each end in 1/1 Rib and remaining sts in stockinette, work even until body measures 12.5 (13.5, 14.5 15.5, 15.5)"/31.75 (34, 36.75, 39, 39 cm) from beg, ending with a WS row.

Join CC. Work ribbing sts in CC, work Row 1 of chart to last 6 sts, work ribbing sts in CC. Work remaining rows of chart, cutting MC after Row 3 and working with CC only from this point.

Join sleeves and body:

Change to longer needle.

Next row (RS): Work across 35 (39, 42, 46, 50) sts, bind off next 12 (16, 20, 22, 24) sts for right underarm, place marker, knit across sts of one sleeve, place marker, knit 71 (79, 85, 93, 101) sts for back, bind off next 12 (16, 20, 22, 24) sts for left underarm, place marker, knit across sts of second sleeve, place marker, work remaining 35 (39, 42, 46, 50) sts - 235 (263, 275, 303, 339) sts. Mark this row at front edge.

Johnnie William Beck is my father.
He continues to mentor and guide me at SWTC.

34

Karaoke Yoked Cardigan *(Cont.)*

Row 2: Rib first and last 6 sts as established, purl rem sts.

Dec Row: [Work to 3 sts before marker, ssk, k1, sl marker, k1, k2tog] 4 times, work to end of row - 8 sts decreased.

Rep last 2 rows once more; rep Row 2 - 219 (247, 259, 287, 323) sts.

Yoke shaping:

Next row (RS): Work to 16 sts beyond left front marker, W&T, work to 16 sts beyond right front marker, W&T.

Rows 3 and 4: Work to 8 sts beyond left front marker, W&T, work to 8 sts beyond right front marker, W&T.

Rows 5 and 6: Work to 4 sts beyond left front marker, W&T, work to 4 sts beyond right front marker, W&T.

Next row: Work across all sts, picking up all wraps and knitting them tog with its parent st.

Work even until yoke measures 4 (4.25, 4.5, 4.75, 5)"/10 (10.75, 11.25, 12, 12.5 cm) above front marker, ending with a WS row. Remove back markers; leave front markers in place.

Dec row 1: Rib 6, knit dec 72 (81, 85, 95, 100) sts evenly, rib 6 - 147 (166, 174, 192, 223) sts.

Work even until yoke measures 6 (6, 6.75, 7, 7.5)"/15.25 (15.25, 17, 17.75, 19 cm) above front marker, ending with a WS row.

Dec row 2: Rib 6, knit dec 49 (55, 57, 63, 70) sts evenly, rib 6 - 98 (111, 117, 129, 153) sts.

Work even until yoke measures 7 (7.5, 8, 8.5, 9)"/17 (19, 20, 22.75 cm) above front marker, ending with a WS row.

Dec Row 3: Rib 6, knit dec 25 (28, 30, 32, 32) sts evenly, rib 6 - 73 (83, 87, 97, 121) sts.

Work 1 row even.

Neck shaping:

Adjust front markers so there are equal amounts of sts on each front.

Next row (RS): Work to 8 sts beyond left front marker, W&T, work to 8 sts beyond right front marker, W&T.

Rows 3 and 4: Work to 6 sts beyond left front marker, W&T, work to 6 sts beyond right front marker, W&T.

Rows 5 and 6: Work to 4 sts beyond left front marker, W&T,

work to 4 sts beyond right front marker, W&T.

Next row: Change to smaller needles. Work across all sts, dec 5 (6, 7, 9, 11) sts evenly in knit area, and picking up all wraps and knitting them tog with its parent st - 68 (77, 81, 89, 109) sts.

Work even in 1/1 Rib for 1 (1, 1, 1.5, 1.5)"/2.5 (2.5, 2.5, 3.75, 3.75 cm)

Bind off in Rib.

Karaoke Yoke Chart

Color Key

MC

CC

Finishing:

Sew sleeve and underarm seams.

Sew in zipper.

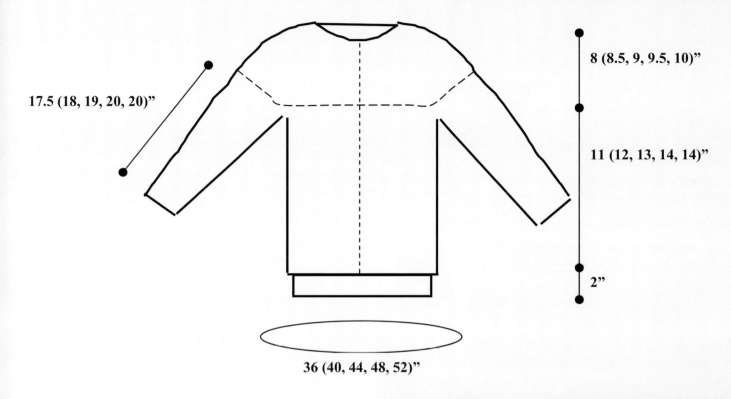

17.5 (18, 19, 20, 20)"

8 (8.5, 9, 9.5, 10)"

11 (12, 13, 14, 14)"

2"

36 (40, 44, 48, 52)"

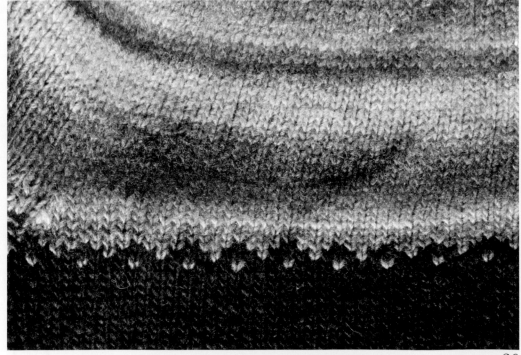

Sophia Learns to Knit

Sophia still beams over her puppets. She recently spent the entire day begging to learn more from Prudence Mapstone during a visit to SWTC. The call to knit is deep in this child.

Sophia, my youngest daughter, has always been intrigued with knitting. On many occasions, she has taken her rightful position as heir to the task of human swift, sitting at my feet helping me make a ball of yarn out of a skein. Being more clever than I am, Sophia will often volunteer her feet instead of her hands, allowing herself to prop her feet up on my chair and still get the job done. From the time she could walk, my spinning wheel was a source of temptation and when she's been meddling with it, the once-threaded projects are left curiously knotted around the spindle. The call to knit is strong in this child.

At five years old, Sophia joined a class in a yarn store near my warehouse. I tried to teach her myself, but Sophia was drawn to formal class... baited by a clever teacher who had promised her a very special project and the companionship of other children learning to knit. She learned to cast on in her first class with a clever story about a rabbit and a tree and by her third class she was knitting her first project. I beamed with pride as she showed me the first four inches she had knit. The piece was a bit longer on the left than the right, and I proudly told her that the dropped stitch was a design element... refusing to utter the words "rip it" that would have rolled quickly from the mouth of my mom.

When we returned the following week, Sophia's teacher had turned her oddly-shaped first project into an adorable finger puppet. Sophia was immensely proud of herself and in love with knitting.

Recently, as we packed for our annual summer trip to my mom's house, Sophia made sure her knitting bag joined mine. This time, she would join my mother and me on the patio in the morning while we knit and chatted together over our first cup of coffee.

Sophia is the first of another generation of women in our family who will carry on the tradition and share our passion for the fiber arts. It is our hope that she will become the guardian of our knitted treasures and see to it that someday her children are swaddled in the handmade blankets and sweaters that we make... and hide safely in the old hope chest.

Sophia's Swatch Puppet

Sophia's Swatch Puppet was a fabulous idea! Every knitting project starts with a swatch to test gauge. I think most of us skip that step, thinking it's just a waste of time. No longer! Turn your swatches into fabulous little puppets to share with the children you love or donate them to any of the wonderful organizations supporting children.

Here's the simple pattern—make your square swatch and check your gauge. I like to make bigger swatches most of the time so I can really get a sense that my gauge works consistently. If you experiment with stitches or needles sizes in the gauge—no problem! It's just a design element for a puppet. With that business aside, fold your swatch in half and sew up the top and side seams, leaving the bottom open for your puppet.

Embellish the puppet anyway you like. Use a crochet hook to create fringe hair, sew on a mouth, sew or glue on wild eyes. We even used old buttons we found in the bottom of a drawer. Scraps of yarn and other fun ideas make this a fun and colorful project. Consider allowing the children to embellish the puppet themselves. Gianna and Sophia delight in choosing the eyes and helping me dream these up. The red puppet quickly became the Sheriff in their puppet show. These little finger puppets provided endless entertainment and inspired them both to keep practicing their knitting… after all as Sophia reminded me, "Seven other fingers need puppets Mom!"

My Love of Hats

My beautiful daughters Gianna (L) and Sophia (R) are my heart and soul. They loved wearing the brain hat. Next on the needles, more brain hats in pink at their request.

As Nona got older, her eyes weakened, making it harder each year to read patterns. To help, my mother and I would sit and read the patterns with her. She would ask questions, look at her lap, and then nod to continue. Much to my amazement, that was all the help she needed. She would quickly remember each pattern, almost as though she could visualize it instantly in her head. Occasionally, she would call for us to stop by and read through a part again or help her modify it so her design was more unique. Her eyes failed, but her skill continued to improve.

The only real difference we noticed was that since Nona was too proud to ask for help often, once she had a pattern in her head, she would make it a lot! There were often variations and subtle differences, but the basic garment showed up in everyone's closet.

In 1984, Nona took advantage of a class taught at the senior center she frequented. The focus on hats inspired over a year of warm winter headgear. In fact, every member of the family had a dresser drawer full of them in no time at all.

While we all enjoyed the hats simply because they looked great and Nona made them, others around Nona received them as gifts when they faced the challenges of cancer. Chemo caps, as they're called, covered the heads of many of Nona's own friends and any friend of the family we learned was facing chemotherapy. The handmade hats were a small act of kindness that helped friends through the hair loss associated with their treatment. Even today, my mother and I carry on this small kindness and make hats, with love, for those who need them. As we craft these pieces, we each say a quiet prayer that this will be the last chemo hat ever needed.

I've always been partial to handmade hats, so Nona's "hat era" was one of my favorites. The only time I hesitated was during her pom-pom binge. I could never get used to those silly balls on the top of my hat. As I write this, I realize that many of the hats and designs Nona made have inspired me, and truth be told, hats are one of my favorite projects to design. Over a dozen of Nona's original hats are still in my dresser drawer. I don't have occasion to wear them often. Arizona winters are very short and mild, but when the temperature drops on those precious cold days, I proudly don those hats and think of Nona.

Among my favorites of the hats that Nona made was the "Brain Warmer," so called for its odd resemblance to the human brain. The simple crochet design is merely a single crochet on the top of the head and then crowded double crochets on a chained "frame", which form the ruffled "brain matter." I have no idea of the origin of this design but we recreated it and updated the look a bit with our favorite yarn, Karaoke.

Ruffled Hat

Skill level: Beginner ◼□□□

Finished size:

Toddler: 16" (color #280, Wild Cherry)

Adult: 20" (color #285, Intensity) with flowers (4 rows mesh)

Adult: 20" (color #281, Bloom) plain (5 rows mesh)

Gauge:

4 sc = 1 inch (2.5 cm)

4 rows = 1 inch (2.5 cm)

Materials:

2 balls SWTC Karaoke (50% Soysilk® fiber/50% wool); [4 MEDIUM]

Stitch marker

G/6/4mm crochet hook

Yarn needle

Notes:

The first part of hat is worked in the round. Use stitch marker to mark the first stitch of each round.

Hat:

Rnd 1:

Ch2, 6 sc in second ch from hook (6 sc).

Rnd 2:

2 sc in each st (12 sc).

Rnd 3:

2 sc in first st, sc in next st, *2 sc, sc in next st, repeat from * around (18 sc).

Rnd 4:

2 sc in first st, sc in next 2 sts, *2 sc, sc in next 2 sts, repeat from * around (24 sc).

Rnd 5:

2 sc in first st, sc in next 3 sts, *2 sc, sc in next 3 sts, repeat from * around (30 sc).

Rnd 6:

2 sc in first st, sc in next 4 sts, *2 sc, sc in next 4 sts, repeat from * around (36 sc).

Rnd 7:

2 sc in first st, sc in next 5 sts, *2 sc, sc in next 5 sts, repeat from * around (42 sc).

Rnd 8:

2 sc in first st, sc in next 6 sts, *2 sc, sc in next 6 sts, repeat from * around (48 sc).

Rnd 9:

2 sc in first st, sc in next 7 sts, *2 sc, sc in next 7 sts, repeat from * around (54 sc).

Rnd 10:

2 sc in first st, sc in next 8 sts, *2 sc, sc in next 8 sts, repeat from * around (60 sc).

Skip to rnd 14 if making toddler hat.

Rnd 11:

2 sc in first st, sc in next 9 sts, *2 sc, sc in next 9 sts, repeat from * around (66 sc).

Rnd 12:

2 sc in first st, sc in next 10 sts, *2 sc, sc in next 10 sts, repeat from * around (72 sc).

Rnd 13:

2 sc in first st, sc in next 11 sts, *2 sc, sc in next 11 sts, repeat from * around (78 sc).

Rnd 14:

Sc in each st around, sl st to marked st. You can now stop using stitch marker (78 sc).

Row 15: Mesh

Ch5, (counts as dc plus ch2) sk2 sts, dc in next st, *ch2, sk2 sts, dc in next st, repeat from * around, sl st to top of third st of starting ch (20/26 ch2 sps).

Row 16:

Repeat row 15.

Row 17:

Repeat row 15.

If making toddler size, skip to row 20.

Please see page 83 for listing of abbreviations.

Row 18:

Repeat row 15.

If making adult size with flowers, skip to row 20.

Row 19:

Repeat row 15.

Row 20: Ruffle

Sl st to first ch2 sp along bottom of hat, ch3, (counts as dc) 3 dc in same sp, 4 dc in each sp around following the diagram below.

This diagram is for the adult version and has 5 mesh rows. For the toddler version there are only 3 mesh rows. For the adult version with flowers there are 4 mesh rows. Work pattern all the way around hat for all sizes. End with a sl st in top of starting ch3.

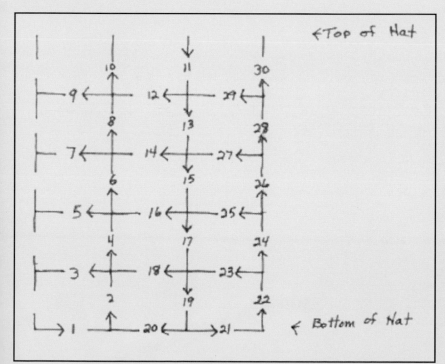

Finishing:

Weave in ends. Make and add embellishments as desired.

Embellishments:

Toddler: Pom Pom

Cut a piece of cardboard 4 inches long by 2 inches high (10 by 5 cm). Wrap yarn around the 2 inch side 50 times. Remove from cardboard and tie in middle. Cut ends to desired length. Sew to top of the hat.

Adult: Flowers (make 5)

Ch5, sl st to form ring, ch 4, sc in ring, *ch3, sc in ring, repeat from * 3 times, (5 ch3 loops), sl st in first ch, sl st in ch3 loop, ch2 (counts as hdc), 6 dc, hdc, in same loop, *hdc, 6 dc, hdc in next loop, repeat from * around, sl st to first st, finish off. Sew just above ruffle putting a 6.5 X 4 mm pony bead in the center. Repeat with rest of flowers.

44

Eufemia's Shawl

*P*erhaps the most exciting gift from the old chest was a shawl hand knit by Eufemia Elvira Maria Benedetti, Nona's mother. Nona first showed it to me when I was a young child, telling me it would someday be mine.

Eufemia was born in Quarazzano, Italy in 1873, the youngest of 5 children. She was a midwife in their small village and the very busy matriarch of her own five-child family. Most of Quarazzano's residents were related and at that time, many of the men left for America in search of a dream. Eufemia's husband was no exception.

Knitting was a necessity for a modest family like the Benedettis. They farmed their land, trading fruit and vegetables for the yarns they needed. The family made what they could from their own resources. Eufemia knit all of the socks, mittens, and sweaters to warm her children during the winter.

When Nona and I would chat about her life in Italy and growing up in Quarazzano, she would sometimes get quiet and reflective. She laughed softly as she told me about her mother and her sisters, bragging that she was a better knitter than all of them. Even as a teenager I would take meticulous notes about Nona's family. By the time she passed away, I had documented her family back 7 generations to the late 1700's.

In the 1980's, Nona returned to Quarazzano with her daughter, Josephine. They spent time with Nona's youngest sister, Elizabetta, and stayed in the family home, which was several hundred years old. Their brother Angelo was also living in Quarazzano along with generations of children and great grandchildren. The siblings hadn't seen each other in 50 years. For Nona and Nonie, it would be the greatest trip of their lives. My own parents visited 10 years later, meeting Elizabetta in her final year.

My mother returned from Italy with a lace bedspread that Elizabetta had made. It was a stunning piece, crocheted meticulously with a very fine thread. We all stood around in awe of the workmanship and love that went into it. Even in her nineties, sibling rivalry consumed Nona. She studied the lace, the patterns, and construction—within a few years she made each of us one just like it.

Eufemia Elvira Maria Benedettion was my great-great-grandmother who knit the exquisite shawl on the left. This house was her home in Quarazzano, Italy.

Photographs by James A. Derheim, European Focus, Inc.

46

Eufemia's Shawl

Eufemia's shawl was crocheted in Broomstick Lace, a technique that first became popular in the Victorian era. Broomstick lace created a lacy, open shawl that was faster and easier than traditional lace making methods. We recreated it in SWTC Bamboo using the same technique. The bamboo gives the stitch definition and stability. We also updated the shape to a rectangle instead of the traditional triangle shape.

Skill Level: Intermediate ⬛◻◻◻▷

Finished Size:

One size fits most

15 X 60" without fringe

Gauge:

1 broomstick and one sc row = 1.5 inches

8 stitches = 1.5 inches

Materials:

3 balls SWTC Bamboo (100% Bamboo); Lilac #151

Size G/6/4mm crochet hook

US size 50 (25 mm) knitting needle

Yarn needle

Note:

Do not turn work at all.

Shawl:

Ch65, sc in second ch from hook and each remaining ch (64 sc).

Broomstick row:

*Put loop that is on hook onto needle, working left to right go into each st, YO, back through st, and put loop on the needle.

Sc row:

Insert hook from right to left through the first 4 loops, YO and pull through, sl st, 4 sc in same sp, insert into next 4 loops, 4 sc in same sp, repeat across (64 sc).

Repeat from * 45 more times (46 broomstick rows).

Edging:

Rnd 1:

Ch2, working down long side of wrap, 4 sc in side loop, *ch4, 4 sc in next side loop, repeat from * across, ch1.

2 sc in each st, 4 sc in side loop, *ch4, 4 sc in next side loop, repeat from * across, ch2, sc in each st, sl st to first st.

Rnd 2 (only done on first long side of wrap):

Sl st to next st, ch1, sc in same, sc, sk st, 5 bs in ch4 sp, *sk st, sc, sc, sk st, 5 bs in next ch4 sp, repeat from * across, sl st to last st, finish off.

Top edge:

With right side facing you join with a sc, sc in each st until ch4 sp, 3 sc in ch4 sp, repeat across, ch1, working left to right, rsc in same st and each st across, finish off, weave in ends.

Finishing:

Cut 256, 12 inch pieces of Bamboo for fringe on short ends. Holding two strands together, fold fringe in half, insert hook from back and loop fringe through in a lark's head knot.

Please see page 83 for listing of abbreviations.

Jonette's Sailor Sweater

Mother Jonette pictured with her brother Jesse in about 1949. They were born 5 years apart on the exact same day.

My mom and her brother, Jesse, were born four years apart on the exact same day. In a small town, that made the newspaper. I saw the little announcement from the day Jonette was born in an album of clippings my grandmother had saved.

I asked my mom about this picture and her entire expression changed. I expected to hear a story about her sixth birthday or an upcoming holiday. "I remember that sweater!" Mom declared.

I was stunned. This picture was nearly 60 years old and the little sailor-collared sweater was fresh in her mind. Her mother had made it for her, and long after she had grown out of it, the sweater remained in her dresser drawer. She had adored the sweater, and refused to part with it. Sometimes a favorite doll got to wear the little sweater but in the end, it was given to a neighbor family who lost their household possessions when the Napa River flooded one winter.

Nona, my Mom's grandmother, lived in the second house from the river on a small dead end street. The river flooded every winter and even in my childhood, I remember the annual family day at Nona's when we all helped her move furniture from the lower level to safety.

The neighbor family had just moved to Post Street and was not prepared for the rising water. They were safe, but their possessions were lost when the river water crested the bank.

Mom still remembered carrying her sweater along with several hand knit blankets, while her mother and grandmother carried plates of pasta they had prepared and several jars of preserves from their basement stash. Then eight years old, the sweater hadn't fit my mom for years, and many more sweaters had since been knit to replace it, but she still recalled the tinge of jealousy she felt when she saw the little neighbor girl wearing her sweater.

After telling me the story, Mom stared silently at the picture. She was still remembering that day and the little sweater. She handed the picture back to me with a smile and said, "I remember the sweater. I've never forgotten how important it was to the family across the street. It was all they had for that moment and my mom's gifts meant a lot to them. I couldn't wait to learn to knit after that."

When Hurricane Katrina struck Louisiana, it was her idea to rally local knitters and create blankets out of sample swatches we had set aside for our sales team. In all, over 25 blankets were sent to a church group who pledged to deliver them to those in need. From time to time, Mom still anonymously sends donations to knitting charities that make blankets (such as Project Linus) and is always the first to knit a hat or scarf for a friend who needs a bit of cheering up. The little sweater made an imprint on her soul, and it taught her the power that a hand knit gift has.

Jonette's Sailor Sweater

Skill Level: Intermediate ◼◻◻◻

Size: Girls 2 (4, 6) Finished bust measurement: 24 (26, 27)"

Gauge: 24 sts/32 rows = 4" (10 cm) in stockinette

Materials:

4 (5,5) skeins SWTC Pure (100% Soysilk® fiber); color #079 Glacier

US size 5 (3.75 mm) and 6 (4mm) needles or sizes required for gauge

Yarn needle

2 buttons, 5/8"(1.5 cm) diameter

Back:

With smaller needles, cast on 70 (78, 82) sts. Work in k2, p2 rib for 2.5 (3, 4) inches/6.25 (7.5, 10) cm. Change to larger needles. SIZE 2 ONLY: On next row, increase 2 sts evenly across row [72 (78, 82) sts]. Continue in stockinette stitch until piece measures 8 (9.5, 11) inches / 20 (24, 28 cm), ending with a WS row.

Armhole shaping: Bind off 6 (5, 5) sts at beg of next 2 rows. Decrease 1 st each side, every other row 6 (5, 5) times [48 (58, 62) sts].

Work even in stockinette until piece measures 12(14.5, 16.5) inches/30.5 (37, 42) cm, ending with a WS row.

Shoulder/Neck shaping: Bind off 3 (4, 4) sts at beg of next 2 rows, then bind off 3 (4, 5) sts at beg of the next 2 rows. Then bind off 4 (4, 5) sts at beg of the next 2 rows. There remain 28 (34, 34) sts. Bind off remaining 28 (34, 34) sts for back neck.

Front:

Work as for back, and, at the same time, when piece measures 9.5 (11, 11.5) inches/24 (28, 29) cm ending with a WS row, begin placket.

Placket:

Knit to center 8 (8, 8) sts, attach a second ball of yarn, bind off center 8 (8, 8) sts and continue across row in stockinette. Working both sides at once, continue in stockinette until piece measures 11 (13.5, 14) inches / 28 (34, 35.5) cm.

Neck shaping: Working both sides at once, bind off 5 (6, 5) sts at neck edge. Decrease 1 st at each side of neck, every other row 5 (7, 8) times. Work even until piece measures 12 (14.5, 16.5) inches/30 (37, 42) cm.

Shoulder shaping: Work as for back.

Sleeves: (make 2)

With smaller needles, cast on 38 (42, 46) sts. Work in k2 p2 rib until piece measures 2.5 (3, 4) inches/6.25 (7.5, 10) cm. Change to larger needles. Work 2 rows in stockinette, ending with WS row.

Sleeve shaping: Increase 1 st on each side every 6th row 2 (8, 8) times, then every 8th row 3 (1, 2) times [48 (60, 66) sts]. Work even in stockinette until piece measures 10 (12, 13) inches/25 (30, 33) cm.

Cap shaping: Bind off 6(5, 5) sts at beg of next 2 rows. Decrease 1 st each side every other row 6 (5, 5) times [24 (40, 46) sts]. Decrease 1 st each side every row 2 (10, 12) times [20 (20, 22) sts]. Bind off 2 sts at the beg of the next 4 rows. Bind off remaining 12 (12, 14) sts.

Finishing:

Sew shoulder seams. Attach sleeves and seam. Seam sides.

Neck finishing: With RS facing and smaller needles, pick up and knit 66 (74, 82) sts, starting from bound off sts above placket, around neck decreases, back neck, and back to bound off sts above placket on opposite side (do not pick up sts in placket yet). Work in k2 p2 ribbing for 1 inch, starting and ending each RS row with k2. Change to larger needles and continue in rib for 2 (3, 3) inches/5 (7.5, 7.5) cm more. Bind off in pattern.

Placket finishing: Button band:

With RS facing, pick up and knit 14(14, 18) sts along left front side of placket. Work in k2 p2 ribbing for 1.5 inches (3.75 cm), starting and ending each RS row with K2. Bind off in pattern. Keep track of number of rows worked.

Buttonhole band (right front): Work as for left front until you have half as many rows, minus 1, as the button band.

Next row (RS): Work 2 (2, 3) sts in pattern, bind off 3 sts, work in pattern to last 5 (5, 6) sts, bind off 3 sts, work 2 (2, 3) sts in pattern.

Next row: Working in pattern, cast on 3 sts over each set of bind off sts.

Complete band as for left front. Sew lower edges of placket bands to bound off stitches at bottom of placket, lapping the buttonhole band over the button band.

Weave in all ends. Sew buttons to button band, opposite buttonholes.

Please see page 83 for listing of abbreviations.

*Gianna is my outdoor kid. She is the happiest running
in the yard and playing with the animals.*

52

The Graduation Shawl

_Jonette Ann Pittore, my mother,
leaving for her graduation._

My mother, Jonette, graduated from high school in 1962. She was a beautiful girl, compared often to her idol, Liz Taylor, for her dark hair and bright green eyes. She was a cheerleader and a good student. She met my father, Johnnie Beck, in her senior year. He was a handsome young man, four years her senior. They met cruising between the two local burger stands one summer night. Jonette was with a group of her girlfriends and Johnnie was with one of his buddies. One of the girls knew both of the boys and introduced them. The group got sodas and fries and spent the evening hanging out together. Later, Johnnie drove Jonette home and asked her out to a show the next night.

Her family was of modest means and often, being "in fashion" meant a good copy. For most of her life, special garments were handmade, hand knit, and hand-me-down. It was a time when young girls could wear these homemade originals with pride and Jonette was fortunate to have a mother who both loved to sew and also remodel clothes to be identical to the "store bought stuff."

Jonette had seen a beautiful shawl in a magazine. It was made of an exotic material or fur that she could not identify, but she loved the style and knew it would add a glamorous, sophisticated touch to anything she might wear at her graduation. So, she asked Nona if she could make her something that looked similar. With the picture in hand, the two designed a pattern so close to the picture that she was sure it would be perfect. Made with love, it would be a graduation present from Nona, her grandmother.

Now, all they needed was a beautiful yarn... but Jonette's vision for her special shawl was far beyond their budget. When they went to the yarn store, Jonette instantly fell in love with the most beautiful yarn in the store—a rich black mohair that was soft and elegant, with a price beyond anything Nona could afford. It had to be from that yarn and Jonette knew it. She told Nona that knitting the shawl would be a huge gift. "I have a job and I will buy the yarn on my next payday," she told Nona proudly. Nona, by then retired and of very limited means, agreed and said that she would give her $20 towards the yarn—Jonette could pay for the rest.

The shawl graced her shoulders above a beautiful dress that Jonette's mother had sewn for her. With her handsome new boyfriend, who would become her life's companion, it made for a most memorable high school graduation. They were married that November, now 44 years ago.

Redux Graduation Wrap

This quick-to-knit wrap features short row shaping, a box pleat in the back, and coordinating buckle closure.

Skill Level: Intermediate ■■■□

Size: One size fits most

Finished circumference: 48" around lower edge

Finished length: 14" at widest point

Materials:

6 balls SWTC Karaoke (50% Soysilk® fiber/50% wool); #279 Black Sheep

US size 11 (8 mm) and 9 (5.5 mm) needles or sizes required for gauge

Size I/9/5.5mm crochet hook

Yarn needle

Circular belt buckle with center post, approximately 2 inches in diameter

Gauge: 12 sts & 16 rows = 4" (10 cm) in stockinette

Wrap and Turn:

Move yarn between needles (to front if you just knit a stitch, to back if you just purled), slip next st, move yarn back, turn piece, slip st back to other needle.

Wrap:

With double strand of yarn and larger needles, cast on 144 sts.

Rows 1-4: Work in garter stitch, ending with WS row.

Short row shaping:

Row 5 (RS): Knit to last 6 sts, wrap and turn.

Row 6: Purl to last 6 sts, wrap and turn.

Rows 7 and 8: As for Rows 5 and 6, except work to last 12 sts.

Rows 9 and 10: As for Rows 5 and 6, except work to last 18 sts.

Rows 11 and 12: As for Rows 5 and 6, except work to last 24 sts.

Rows 13 and 14: As for Rows 5 and 6, except work to last 30 sts.

Rows 15 and 16: As for Rows 5 and 6, except work to last 36 sts.

Rows 17 and 18: As for Rows 5 and 6, except work to last 42 sts.

Rows 19 and 20: As for Rows 5 and 6, except work to last 48 sts.

Rows 21 and 22: Knit across, picking up and knitting all wraps together with the appropriate stitch.

Rows 23 and 24: Work in garter stitch.

Rows 25-32: Continue in stockinette, knitting 1st and last 5 sts on all WS rows to maintain a garter st border.

Rows 33-36: Work in garter stitch.

Row 37 (decrease row): *K10, k2tog; rep from * across (132 sts).

Row 38: K5, purl to last 5 sts, k5.

Rows 39-58: Repeat rows 5-24.

Bind off all stitches.

Box Pleat:

Find center point along top edge of wrap. Measure 6" (15.25 cm) to the left and right of center point and mark. Fold marks in to center point, pin to secure. With crochet hook and single strand of yarn, work 1 row of single crochet along bound off edge, working through all thicknesses along pleats. Secure yarn at end.

Front closure:

Left front:

With double strand of yarn, smaller needles, and RS facing, pick up and knit 21 sts along the left side of the wrap (as it would be worn).

Next row: Sl1, *k1, p1; rep from * across.

Continue working in k1 p1 rib, slipping the first st of each row, until piece is 1 inch long, ending with a WS row.

Next row: Sl1, *k2tog; rep from * across [11 sts].

Continue in k1 p1 rib as before, slipping first st of each row, until piece measures 3" (7.5 cm). Bind off.

Right front:

Work as for left front, except continue in k1 p1 (on 11 sts) until piece measures 6 inches. Bind off.

Finishing:

With double strand of yarn and crochet hook, work single crochet around outside edge of belt buckle to cover.

Wrap the shorter (left front) strap around center post of buckle and sew firmly to secure (the 2" [5 cm] long, narrow portion of the strap should be used). Weave in ends and block.

Please see page 83 for listing of abbreviations.

Mom is still my best friend. We talk daily and share the responsibility for SWTC.

The Cardigan Sweater

Seeing Nona in the corner of the room knitting was a familiar sight. Even now when I close my eyes and think of her, this is the vision I see"

In the front of Nona's house was a large, cedar-lined closet. Over the years, the entire family had stored extra clothes there. The cedar lining protected our favorite knit garments, blankets and other treasured clothes from moths and other potential hazards. Little did we know, the big closet was like a private yarn store to Nona. Over the years, she had shopped the closet to pick out old sweaters, carefully unwinding, skeining, and washing the yarns to straighten them, finally recycling them into new and more modern apparel. She was amazingly thrifty.

I last visited the closet when Nona moved from her house to live with my parents. I stood quietly on a gold rug in the center of the closet intrigued by all of the things that had been stuffed into it over the years. The silence was shattered when my mother walked in and shrieked, startling the senses out of me. I began laughing so hard that I had to wipe the tears from my eyes as Mom stared at the gold rug—realizing it was her favorite hand knit coat recycled. It was then I understood where all of her cardigan sweaters had gone— they were now coat hangers, baby blankets and little pillows. The one in the picture became over a dozen pair of slippers one Christmas.

In the few pictures we have of Nona, she is always wearing her trademark cardigan sweater. Sometimes the design was inspired from a commercial pattern or simply seeing some-one wearing a sweater she admired. On occasion, she would tackle complex Aran designs or heavily cabled pieces—but her favorite garments were the simplest. Most often, she worked from a basic pattern she had memorized and then made subtle changes to make the particular garment special. A unique cable added to the front or a pattern stitch in the bands changed the design completely. Nona always loved the simplicity of a cardigan both in their wear and design.

We never found any of Nona's cardigans but could identify the recycled things they later became. It was a game to recall which sweater the little slippers and hangers had originally been. Tucked away in a large tattered box, I found the yarn I had used in the first sweater that I knitted. I had stored it in the cedar closet when I left for college. Nona transformed the little sweater, which had one sleeve slightly longer than the other, into a pillow.

Nona's Cardigan Sweater

Here we recreated Nona's basic cardigan from SWTC Karaoke. In Nona's own tradition, the basic pattern is a template for endless variations. Some ideas are shared here. Consider the possibilities that come from subtle variations in the rib stitches, varying the yarn colors or adding simple cables. You will become the artist and designer with this basic template.

This sweater is knit in one piece. Sleeves are attached at the armholes.

Skill Level: Easy ■■□□

Finished bust measurement: 38" (42", 46", 48", 52")

Gauge: 4.5 sts & 6 rows = 1" in pattern stitch on larger needles

Materials:

9 (10, 11, 13, 14) balls SWTC Karaoke (50% Soysilk® fiber/ 50% wool); #282 Forest

US size 5 (3.75 mm) and 8 (5 mm) circular knitting needles in 16", 24", 32" lengths and US size 5 double-pointed needles, or sizes required for gauge

1 - 22" separating zipper

Body:

With smaller needles, cast on 171 (189, 207, 225, 243) sts. DO NOT JOIN.

1. (K1, p1) repeat ending with k1.

2. (P1, k1) repeat ending with p1.

Repeat these 2 rows for 3" for all sizes.

Change to larger needles and continue to work in St st (knit 1 row, purl 1 row) inc 1 st in the center on the first row only (172 (190, 208, 226, 244) sts. Work until piece measures 15" (15", 16", 16", 17") from beginning. End by working a right side row.

Divide for Fronts and Back:

With wrong side facing, purl 38 (42, 46, 50, 54) sts. Bind off 10 (10, 12, 13, 14) sts, purl across 74 (86, 92, 100, 108) sts, Bind off 10 (10, 12, 13, 14) sts, purl 38 (42, 46, 50, 54) sts and set aside.

Sleeves:

With smaller dpns, cast on 42 (46, 48, 48, 52) sts. Place marker and join, being careful not to twist your stitches. Working onto smaller needles, k1, p1 for 2.5" (2.5", 3", 3". 3.5"). Change to larger needles and St st (knit all rounds). At the same time, inc

59

1 st before and 1 st after the marker every 6 rounds until there are 64 (72, 76, 80, 86) sts. When sleeve measures 15.25" (17", 17.5", 18", 18.5") from the beginning or desired length to underarm stop 5 (5, 6, 7, 8) sts before marker. Bind off 10 (10, 12, 13, 14) sts remember to remove marker when you get to it. Make 1 more sleeve to match.

Joining Sleeves to Body:

Starting with body and RS facing, knit across 38 (43, 46, 48, 52) sts of right front, pm, knit across 54 (62, 63, 67, 72) sts of first sleeve, pm, knit across 76 (86, 92, 96, 104) sts of back, pm, knit across 54(62, 63, 67, 72) sts of second sleeve, pm, knit across 38 (43, 46, 48, 52) sts of left front. There will be a total of 260 (296, 310, 326, 352) sts. Purl next row. Work 2 rows in St st.

Shaping:

Knit to 3 sts before marker, ssk, k1, sm, k1, k2tog. Repeat across row for all markers. Purl back.

Repeat decrease every 2nd row 20 (25, 25, 27, 31) times,

At the same time, when the piece measures 6.5" (7.25", 7.25", 7.5", 8") from joining round, shape crew neck as follows:

Continuing raglan decreasing, bind off at the beg of next 2 rows 5 (5, 7, 7, 8) sts.

Bind off 3 sts at neck edge 1 (2, 2, 2, 2) times.

Bind off sts at neck edge 3 (2, 2, 2, 3) times.

Bind off 1 st at neck edge every RS row 1 (2, 3, 3, 2) times. After all decreases are complete, put remaining 38 (46, 46, 54, 56) sts on a holder.

Neckband:

With RS facing, pick up 20 sts up left slope, knit remaining sts left on hold, pick up 20 sts down right slope.

WS: *P1, k1* end with p1.

RS: *K1, p1* end with k1.

Repeat for 1 inch, bind off using larger needle.

Finishing:

Fold back bottom rib and cuffs and sew down. Position zipper, pin down and sew in place using needle and thread. Weave in all ends and sew underarm seams.

Please see page 83 for listing of abbreviations.

This Cardigan sweater, knit in SWTC Karaoke is comfy and roomy.

The Hangers

My mother Jonette got this big box of hangers for Christmas in 1973. She still has most of them in her closet.

I went to a garage sale in Chandler, Arizona last year—in the pile of once-loved things were 7 hangers, all hand crocheted. The lady hosting the sale saw me grab them out of the pile and yelled across the lawn that they were 5 cents each. I stood staring at them, imagining who made them and how they could possibly be discarded at a garage sale. The stitches were even and well done. They were knit in a fine quality, expensive wool yarn. I gathered them all up, paid the 35 cents and took them home. Somebody had made them with love, and I couldn't leave them behind.

Growing up, I had a closet full of brightly colored clothes hangers. Some were knit, others crocheted. As a child, I loved how soft they were and the fun colors they were made in. I also loved that my clothes didn't fall off, making my closet messy and getting me in trouble. Many of those hangers are still in my closet today... and in my sister's closet... and in my mother's closet. If they were all gathered together, we would probably have hundreds of them.

My grandmothers made the hangers at their knitting circle when they would join other ladies at the senior center. Often times, the entire group of knitters prepared hangers for charity sales, donation, or just made them for their own families. They would trade finished hangers with each other, share patterns, and enjoy each other's company.

Mom and I bought hangers whenever we could to make sure Nonie and Nona had enough supplies for their projects. They were very thrifty and would never allow us to spend money on them, so we always took off the tags and told them someone gave us the hangers or that we had them in our closets. We would often do the same with yarn—buying fine boutique yarns, removing the price tags, and presenting them with grand stories about finding them in the bargain bin at a nearby thrift shop. Loving a great deal, Nonie and Nona would be thrilled to crochet with wonderful yarns, knowing they were such a bargain. Mom and I were always pleased with how convincing we could be—and never minded the little white lies since it made these special ladies so happy.

Nonie and Nona used remnants of yarn from other projects to make the hangers. They never wasted even a small piece of yarn. The decorated hangers were really a spectacular idea. They protect special garments from saggy shoulders, make great gifts and are easy and quick to make.

Hangers

Covered hangers keep fine garments in good shape and off the closet floor. Slipping the first stitch on all rows gives you a nice edge for finishing. And for a little extra fun, try inserting a little lavender before you finish seaming the cover onto the hanger!

Skill level: Easy ◖■□◗

Finished size: to fit average hanger

Gauge: 5 sts and 6 rows = 1 inch (2.54 cm)

Materials:

1 ball SWTC Karaoke (50% Soysilk® fiber/50% wool)

US size 7(4.5 mm) straight and double-pointed needles or size required for gauge

1 stitch marker

1 plastic hanger

Hanger:

Cast on 16 leaving long tail.

Row 1: Purl across row.

Row 2: Knit across row.

Row 3: Purl across row.

Row 4: Knit 6 sts, inc 1 in next sts, place marker, inc 1 st in next stitch again, knit to end (18 sts).

Row 5: Purl.

Row 6: *Knit across row.

Row 7: Purl across row.

Row 8: Knit row. Increase in the stitch before and the stitch after marker, knit to end (20 sts).

Next: Purl across row* Repeat * * until you have 40 sts.

Next: Purl across row.

Next: Knit across row.

Next: Purl across row.

Make hole for hanger:

Row 1: Knit 20, remove marker, k2tog, place marker YO, knit to end (40 sts).

Row 2: Purl across row.

Row 3: Knit across row.

Row 4: Purl across row.

Row 5: Knit 18, place marker, k2tog, sl1, k1, psso, knit to end (38 sts).

Row 6: *Purl across row.

Row 7: Knit across row.

Row 8: Purl across row.

Row 9: Knit to marker, k2tog, k1, sl1, k1, psso, knit to end.* Repeat from * to * until you have 16 sts.

Next: Purl across row.

Next: Knit across row.

Next: Purl across row.

Bind off. With right side out put hook of hanger through hole and seam up sides and bottom. Weave in ends.

Cast on 6 sts using size 4 dpns, make 1 cord the length of the hook from tip to neck. Cast off, slip over hook, and hand stitch to body of hanger for a great finish!

Please see page 83 for listing of abbreviations.

We Celebrate Christmas

*Jonna, my sister was born in 1967, I am in the red dress.
From left, Nona (holding Jonna), proud mother Jonette,
and Nonie on the right.*

We love to celebrate Christmas. It's a very special time to gather and honor our family and friendships. Our family was small, but the holidays brought us all home, and often, brought treasured family friends without family nearby also. There was a place at our table for everyone and it was always the highlight of our year.

The holiday season kicked off in early November when the women gathered to make ravioli, a traditional Italian pasta. It was a weekend-long event and each lady, young and old, had a job. Nona was head chef and everyone else dutifully took her direction—someone rolled dough, someone pressed and cut. My sister and I loved Ravioli Day and had a critical job—we stuffed the ravioli. It was also our honor to taste and approve the first ravioli each year. I loved that part. On ravioli weekend, we made enough for Thanksgiving and Christmas dinner too—sometimes twenty or thirty dozen. When the work was done, there was one other tradition to uphold. Out came the tape measure and my little sister and I were fitted for all of the new things that would be knit for us before Christmas. At the end of the day, Nona, Nonie, and Mom would collapse on the couches and knit for a while before we went home. They wouldn't finish their marathon knitting until every member of the family had something new for Christmas.

Over the years, one of the greatest traditions to stem from this was a love and deep respect for a handmade gift. In my earliest memories, Mom spent the weeks before Christmas teaching us a new craft or helping us make some special gift for every member of our family. From early years of just drawing pictures to a tray of baked cookies and eventually to larger and more creative projects, we embraced the artistry and creativity. Once I learned to knit, I loved to make scarves or hats for everyone! In lean years, when money was tight, handmade gifts were sometimes the only ones under the tree and that was just wonderful. Many of our dresses were hand sewn and our sweaters were all hand knit. I wouldn't have had it any other way. I remember my freshman year in college; I bought gifts for everyone and didn't have time to make even one thing. I hated that year… it just wasn't the same. I missed the pride and excitement of giving something I had made.

This is me at age 2 in a knit dress.

When I was looking for pictures to include in this book, I found the picture of my mother in her soft green cowl neck dress. It was 1967 and I was just two years old. She remembered it clearly… it was one of the lean years. That lovely dress had been knit by Nonie for her to wear for the holidays. My sister had been born in October, and as any young new mother has experienced, money and time were tight. Her mother knew that the dress would make this young Mom feel wonderful through the holidays, and it did.

With the help of one of my favorite knitwear designers, Diane Zangl, we created a cowl neck sweater for our 2006 collection, which we share here. The yarn, called Gianna, was named for my first daughter, Gianna Marie and is modeled by my mother, Jonette. As I write this, the holidays are fast approaching. Beside me is a basket of yarn, waiting impatiently to become hats and scarves. We all live in Arizona now and it's likely it will be 70 degrees on Christmas day, but everyone will have a new hat or scarf. I will tell them all about my grandmothers who taught me how to knit, the ornaments on the tree honoring something special each year, and the special gifts I knit for them. We don't make our ravioli by hand anymore, but they will still grace our table and my daughters will have the honor of tasting the first ones.

The Cowl Collar Sweater

A winding cable flows from a rib into the body, and is featured front and center on this slightly oversized pullover. Portions of the cable are repeated on the modified set-in sleeves, while a cowl collar completes the classic look.

Skill Level: Intermediate ■■■◻

Size: Woman's S (M, L, XL)

Instructions are given for smallest size, with larger sizes in parentheses. When only one number is given, it applies to all sizes.

Finished Measurements:

Chest: 36 (40, 44, 48)"/91 (102, 112, 122) cm

Side to underarm: 14 (14, 15, 15.5)"/35.5 (35.5, 38, 39) cm

Armhole depth: 7.5 (8, 8.5, 9)"/19 (20, 21.5, 23) cm

Sleeve length: 18 (18, 18.5, 18.5)"/46 (46, 47, 47) cm

Gauge: 12 sts and 17 rows = 4" (10 cm) in stockinette

Front/back panel = 5.5" (14 cm)

Sleeve panel = 6" (14.25 cm)

Materials:

18 (18, 20, 21) balls SWTC Gianna (50% Soysilk® fiber/ 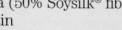 50% Wool); color #039 Falling Rain

US size 10.5 (6.5 mm) straight and 16" (41 cm) circular needles, or size required for gauge.

Cable needle

Stitch markers

Notes:

For sleeve pattern, work Rows 1-4 only of chart.

When collar is folded over, knit sts will face outwards.

Back:

CO 60 (68, 76, 84) sts. Mark center 28 sts.

Set up pattern (WS): *K1, p3; rep from * to marker, k1, p6, [k4, p6] twice, k1, [p3, k1] to end of row.

Next Row: *P1, k3; rep from * to marker, work

Row 1 of chart over next 28 sts, [k3, p1] to end of row.

Keeping sts between markers in chart pat, and remaining sts in

3/1 Rib as established, work even until rib measures 2.5", ending with a WS row.

Next Row (RS): Knit to marker inc 2 (1, 0, 0) sts evenly spaced, work established cable pat over next

28 sts, knit to end of row inc 2 (1, 0, 0) sts evenly spaced – 64 (70, 76, 84) sts.

Keeping sts between markers in established cable pat, and remaining sts in stockinette, work even until back measures 14 (14, 15, 15.5)" from beg, ending with a WS row.

Shape underarm:

Bind off 6 (6, 7, 8) sts at beg of next 2 rows. Dec 1 st each end every RS row 2 (3, 4, 4) times – 48 (52, 54, 60) sts.

Work even until armhole measures 7.5 (8, 8.5, 9)"/19 (20, 21.5, 23) cm above bound-off underarm sts, ending with a WS row.

Shape shoulders and back neck

Mark center 26 (28, 30, 32) sts.

Next Row (RS): Knit to marker, join second ball of yarn and bind off marked center sts, knit to end of row. 11 (12, 12, 14) sts each side.

Working on both sides of neck with separate balls of yarn, dec 1 st at each neck edge every row twice, at the same time bind off at each arm edge 4 (5, 5, 6) sts once, then 5 (5, 5, 6) sts once.

Front:

Work as for back until front measures 4.5 (5, 5, 5.5)"/11.25 (12.5, 12.5, 14) cm above bound-off underarm sts, ending with a WS row. Mark center 24 (26, 28, 30) sts.

Next Row (RS): Knit to marker, join second ball of yarn and bind off marked center sts, knit to end of row. – 12 (13, 13, 15) sts each side.

Working on both sides of neck with separate balls of yarn, dec 1 st at each neck edge every RS row 3 times.

Work even until armhole measures same as for back above bound-off underarm sts. Shape shoulders as for back.

Sew shoulder seams.

Please see page 83 for listing of abbreviations.

Jonette still loves cowl neck sweaters. Splitting her time between Napa, Ca and Phoenix, AZ means she still has opportunities for brisk winter days and cool evenings.

Cowl Collar Sweater

Collar:

With circular needle and RS facing, beg at shoulder seam, pick up and knit 3 sts for every 4 rows along sides of neck, and 1 st in every bound-off st of center front and back neck. Join, placing marker between first and last st.

Work even in reverse stockinette (purl every rnd) until collar measures 2". Inc on next rnd, if necessary, to bring multiple of sts to a number divisible by 4. Continue to work even until collar measures 8".

Ribbing Rnd: *K1, p3; rep from * around.

Rep Ribbing Rnd twice more.

Bind off loosely in pat.

Sleeves:

With smaller needles, cast on 32 (34, 36, 38) sts. Mark center 28 sts.

Set up pattern (WS):

Size small only: P2, k1, p6, [k4, p6] twice, k1, p2.

Size medium only: P3, k1, p6, [k4, p6] twice, k1, p3.

Size large only: K1, p3, k1, p6, [k4, p6] twice, k1, p3, k1.

Size extra-large only: P1, k1, p3, k1, p6, [k4, p6] twice, k1, p3, k1, p1.

Keeping sts between markers in Rows 1 through 4 only of chart pat, and remaining sts in 3/1 Rib as established, work even until rib measures 3", ending with a WS row.

Next Row (RS): Knit to marker, work established cable pat over next 28 sts, knit to end of row.

Keeping sts between markers in established cable pat and rem sts in Stockinette, inc 1 st each end every 4th row 11 (11, 12, 12) times – 54 (56, 60, 62) sts.

Work even until sleeve measures 18 (18, 18.5, 18.5)"/46 (46, 47, 47) cm, ending with a WS row. Mark each end st for underarm.

Shape sleeve cap:

Continue to work even for 6 (6, 6, 8) rows more.

Dec 1 st each end every RS row 2 (3, 4, 4) times.

Bind off rem 50 (50, 52, 54) sts.

69

Finishing:

Sew sleeves into armholes, matching underarm markers to first bound-off st of underarm.

Sew sleeve and side seams.

Jonette loves this sweater both for the design and because its made from the yarn named after her first grandchild, GIANNA.

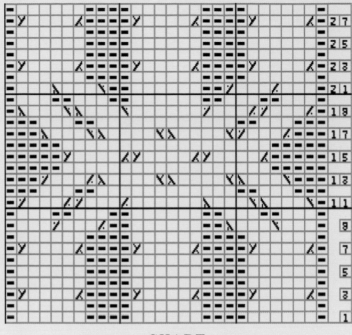

CHART
GIANNA PULLOVER

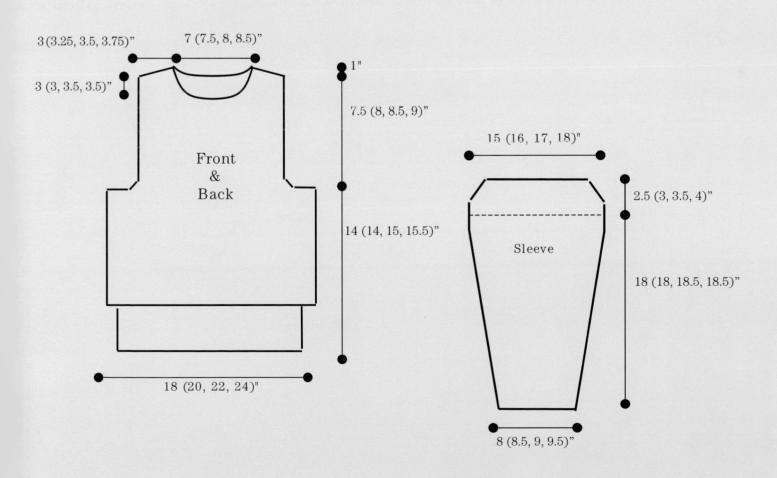

3 (3.25, 3.5, 3.75)"

7 (7.5, 8, 8.5)"

3 (3, 3.5, 3.5)"

1"

7.5 (8, 8.5, 9)"

Front
&
Back

14 (14, 15, 15.5)"

18 (20, 22, 24)"

15 (16, 17, 18)"

2.5 (3, 3.5, 4)"

Sleeve

18 (18, 18.5, 18.5)"

8 (8.5, 9, 9.5)"

If You Are So Tired, Why Are You Knitting?

Gianna wearing the sporty little cardigan designed just for her with her Nonie, my mother Jonette.

"If you are so tired, why are you knitting?" I had missed Gianna's soccer practice and she was quite angry.

After a particularly difficult work week and a losing battle with a very bad cold, that simple sentence pierced through me. There was no fight left in me—just sadness that my few available minutes of Mommy time were under attack.

I think every working mom is a superhero. We struggle to balance the demands of work, home, and all of our children's sports, clubs, events and activities. Busy moms can direct a child to a missing shoe without even looking for it, and sense closet clutter through a closed door. My superhero cape may be knit, but like all superhero moms, I work too many hours and replace sleep and healthy eating with coffee. Sometimes, I just need a break, and knitting is my time out.

But how do you explain the importance of knitting to a seven year old?

I put my knitting aside and gave my angry child a big hug, drawing her to my lap for a chat. I apologized for missing practice and assured her that I would be at every game and practice I could. After some discussion, we seemed to have an understanding.

It was time to talk about my knitting.

I gathered Gianna and Sophia for a bedtime story about my grandmothers' magic hope chest. The hope chest is a tradition in our family that will continue with them. There is a cedar-lined chest for each daughter in my room, guarding many of the hand-knit treasures already made for them and the gifts that would someday warm their own children. We talked about knitting and how special it was to the women of our family, as well as how meaningful it continues to be for me. They were reminded that our sheep, goats, and llamas would grow long coats we would spin into yarn, and then knit into hats for winter. Gianna asked endless questions about Nona and Nonie. She had seen their pictures before, but tonight, they seemed to come alive in her imagination and captivate her curiosity.

Through my story, the girls realized that I knit to relax, to express love through my gifts, and to feel connected with my family. I knit to create a legacy for my daughters and for their future children. I explained that for me, knitting isn't more important than soccer practice, it was how I relax, and that, with my knitting, I create things for the people I love. The girls suddenly realized that every year they receive new handmade sweaters, hats, and scarves. Their drawers were full of hand-knits. That was a lot of love!

We talked and laughed for hours as I shared stories about our family. Now way past bedtime, Sophia had fallen asleep and Gianna was struggling to keep her eyes open, but as she started to doze off she whispered, "Mom, will you teach me to knit tomorrow?"

I returned to my knitting and worked into the morning hours finishing another cardigan sweater for my daughters. This had been a wonderful evening and I couldn't wait to spend the next day knitting with Gianna. I learned a lesson, too. Next week, no matter what, you will find me on the sidelines at soccer practice, cheering on Gianna and Sophia and knitting while I watch.

Gianna's most recent sweater was a sporty pink cardigan that ties in the front and has a great design on the back. This sweater means more to her than ones she's had in the past. After a few hours of knitting lessons she realizes there's a lot more to making a sweater than meets the eye.

Gianna's Fabulous Cardigan

Skill level: Intermediate ■■■□

Size: Girls 6-7 (8-9, 10-12)

Gauge:

18 st and 25 rows to 4" (10 cm) square in stockinette on larger needles.

Materials:

4 (5, 6) balls SWTC Phoenix (100% Soysilk® fiber); #090 [4 MEDIUM]

US size 9 (5.5 mm) needles and 10 (6 mm) needles or sizes required for gauge

Cable needle if desired

1 yard each leather strip in dark brown and/or pink suede (alternately, use 1 inch strips of organza)

4 each natural coconut wood circular beads

Yarn needle

Notes:

This garment has selvedge stitches to facilitate sewing up. Selvedge stitches are not included in the stitch count.

All edges are self-finished, please join yarn in side or underarm seams to ensure neat finish.

Back:

Cast on 60 (65, 70) st plus 2 selv st using smaller needles.

Start Rib:

1st row: Selv, * k2, p3 * rib rep till end, selv.

2nd row and all alternate rib rows: Selv, * k3 p2 * rep till end, selv.

3rd row: Selv, * C2R, p3 * rib rep till end, selv.

4th row: as 2nd row.

Rep these 4 rows twice, and 1st and 2nd rows once more. Total 14 rows.

Change to larger needles.

Knit in St st for 10 rows.

Begin Chart, making sure to center the motif.

Work following chart until work measures 26 (28,30) cm from cast on.

Please note: Armholes begin before the chart is completed.

Armholes:

At beg of next 2 rows, bind off 3 sts.

3rd Row: Selv, k1, k2tog, knit to last 3 sts, ssk, k1, selv.

4th row: Selv, p to end, selv.

Rep last 2 rows twice more.

Cont in St st for 34 (39, 44) rows.

Next row for back neck:

Selv, k16 (17, 19), bind off 16 (17, 20) st neatly, k16 (17, 19) selv.

Leave live sts on stitch holders for 3 needle bind off of shoulders when fronts are completed.

Left front:

Cast on 33 (35, 37) plus 2 selv sts using smaller needles.

Start Rib:

1st row: Selv, * k2, p3 * rib rep till end, selv.

2nd row and all alternate rib rows: Selv, * k3, p2 * rep till end, selv.

3rd row: Selv, * C2R, p3 * rib rep till end, selv.

4th row: as 2nd row.

Rep these 4 rows twice, and 1st and 2nd rows once more. Total 14 rows.

Change to larger needles.

Start Cable and Lace Front.

Row 1: Selv, knit to last 5 sts, ssk, YO, C2R, k1, selv.

Row 2 and all even rows till neck shaping: Selv, p to end, selv.

Rep these 2 rows until work measures 26 (28, 30) cm from cast on.

Armholes:

At beg of next row, bind off 3 sts, cont as set for front cable and lace.

Please see page 83 for listing of abbreviations.

2nd Row: Selv, p to end, selv.

3rd Row: Selv, k1, k2tog, knit to last 5 st, ssk, YO, C2R, k1, selv.

4th row: Selv, p to end, selv.

Rep rows 3 and 4 another 3 times.

Neck shaping:

Row 1: Selv, k to last 5 st, ssk, C2R, k1, selv.

Please note: YO has been left out on purpose.

Row 2: Selv, p to end, selv.

Rep these 2 rows 9 (10, 10) times more. 16 (17, 19) st rem.

Right front:

Knit as for Left front, reversing all shaping.

Cable and lace for Left front:

Row 1: Selv, k1, C2R, YO, ssk, k to end, selv.

Row 2: and all even rows till neck shaping: Selv, p to end, selv.

3 needle bind off shoulders.

Sleeves: Make 2

Cast on 33 (35, 37) st plus 2 selv st using smaller needles.

Start Rib:

1st row: Selv, * k2, p3 * rib rep till end, selv.

2nd row and all alternate rib rows: Selv, * ,k3, p2 * rep till end, selv.

3rd row: Selv, * C2R, p3 * rib rep till end, selv.

4th row: as 2nd row.

Rep these 4 rows twice, and 1st and 2nd rows once more. Total 14 rows.

Change to 6 mm needles.

Knit in St st for 10 rows.

Increasing:

1st row: Selv, k2, M1, knit to last 3 st, M1, k2, selv.

2nd row: Selv, p across, selv.

3rd row: Selv, k across, selv.

4th row: Rep row 2.

Increase a total of 9 (11, 12) times. 51 (57, 61) sts.

Decrease for sleeve cap:

Bind off 3 st at beg of next 2 rows.

Dec 1 st on either side of sleeve cap on next 3 RS rows.

Knit 2 rows St st.

Dec 1 st on either side of sleeve cap on next row and every 4th row twice more.

Knit 6 rows St st.

Dec 1 st on either side of sleeve cap on next row.

Knit 4 rows St st.

Bind off 3 st at beg of next 4 rows. 17 (23, 27) sts rem.

Bind off rem sts.

Finishing:

Sew sleeves to fit into armholes.

Sew up side and underarm seams.

Weave in yarn ends.

Attach the leather strip (or organza strips) as shown in pictures, using the smaller beads outside the larger beads to indicate hands and feet.

Using remaining pink suede, tie bows through the YO in the fronts. Alternatively, use cuff links to attach 2 fronts together.

On Sunday, September 9, 2001, my husband Joe and I went out for our evening stroll. Without fail, my two babies always fell asleep within minutes of leaving the house. So, for as long as we walked, Joe and I could reconnect, talk about our day, and just have some quiet moments. Gianna was just 2 years old and my baby, Sophia, was 7 months. Quiet moments were rare.

Joe noticed that something was bothering me on this evening. After some prodding, I reluctantly admitted that I was worried about his business trip the next morning. Joe traveled 7 months out of the year—he flew constantly. But this trip was different. Every time I thought about it, a sense of dread came over me. I couldn't explain myself and had no concrete reason to offer. Joe was willing stay home to ease my worry, but his meeting on Tuesday was with his biggest and most important client. How could I stand in the way?

He left Monday morning for Washington, DC. His flight was ordinary and he called me to say there was nothing to worry about... he was safe. The dread I had felt was still there, but I chalked it up to exhaustion.

On Tuesday, September 11, 2001, my sleep was cut short at just after 7 am. My cell phone started ringing, my house phone was ringing, and someone was pounding on my door. I remember sitting up in bed and feeling a cold, somber fear overwhelm me, and at that moment, I was afraid to move. At the front door, my friend Nina stood with a panicked look and tears in her eyes. She pushed past me and headed for the TV. My babies were crying, and I wrestled to take control of the moment and get my bearings. I raced to the phone, and was instantly relieved to hear Joe's voice. He was terrified... his voice betrayed him. I stood in front of the TV watching breaking news of the terror attacks on the Twin Towers, listening to Joe explain that he had just seen the plane hit the Pentagon in Washington, DC from the window of his client's office.

Like most Americans, those first few hours were filled with horror, fear, and panic. We had no idea what was happening to our country, or why, or even how to react. Since Joe had a rental car, I urged him to leave DC immediately and head for his parents' house in New Jersey until we knew more. Flying wasn't an option, so at least he would be with family while we waited for more information.

I spent the next few days glued to the TV trying to grasp what had happened. My knitting became my sanity. With my babies at my side, I kept my hands and mind busy to ease the fear. I worried about Joe every minute he was away that trip, and knitted a beautiful scarf to give him as soon as he walked in the door.

On September 21, 2001, Joe finally made it home. He had driven to New Jersey, where his father joined him, and the two then made their way to Phoenix by car. I raced outside to greet Joe. The scarf I had knit embodied the entire experience for me and had somehow become my connection to Joe through this tragedy. To this day, the mere sight of it reminds me of 9/11, and I soon dubbed it the HUG Scarf. That day, every American family was reminded to hug their children, their spouses, and their loved ones.

The Hug Scarf

Skill level: Easy ◖■☐▯

Finished size: 8" x 60"

Gauge: 5 sts and 6 rows = 1 inch in pattern on larger needles

Materials:

2 balls SWTC Inspiration (50% Alpaca/50% Soysilk® fiber) 🧶 **3** LIGHT

US size 4 (3.5 mm) and 6 (4 mm) needles or size required for gauge

Yarn needle

Begin:

With smaller needles, cast on 40 sts.

Knit 6 rows.

*Next row: Purl across.

Next row: Knit across *. Repeat from *to* 2 times.

Knit next 7 rows.

Next row: With right side facing and larger needles, * sl1 purlwise with yarn in back, YO, k2tog, repeat from * to end.

Next row: K1, * sl1 purlwise with yarn in back, YO, k2tog, repeat from * to end.

Repeat last 2 rows 4 times.

Knit 1 row.

Pattern:

Switch to smaller needles and knit next 6 rows.

*Next row: Purl across.

Next row: Knit across *. Repeat from * to * 2 times.

Next row: Purl across.

Knit next 5 rows across.

Next row: With right side facing and larger needles, * sl1 purlwise with yarn in back, YO, k2tog, repeat from * to end.

Next row: K1, *sl1 purlwise with yarn in back, YO, k2tog, repeat from * to end.

Repeat last 2 rows 4 times.

Repeat the pattern section 18 times.

Finishing:

*Next row: Purl across.

Next row: Knit across *. Repeat * to * 2 times.

Knit next 7 rows.

*Next row: Purl across.

Next row: Knit across *. Repeat * to * 2 times.

Bind off, weave ends and block.

Please see page 83 for listing of abbreviations.

October 1, 2001...
It Just Couldn't Get Worse.

For the previous eight years, I had worked as a real estate negotiator in telecom. Like my parents, I traveled around the country, working as part of a team to build the systems that make cell phones work. It was the job of my dreams! I loved the travel, the money, the lifestyle. After meeting my husband and settling down to start a family, I retired from the road and left the travel to him. I've never been one to sit idle, and quickly found myself with a fledgling recruiting firm to supply staff back to the companies I had worked for in the past. Joe continued in telecom, and worked his way to a VP position for a struggling engineering firm making a salary that was absurdly generous. We were quite proud of his achievements.

When the planes crashed, the stock market crashed... telecom crashed... and Joe's firm closed its doors. My recruiting business screeched to a halt as the development projects reacted to the American financial crisis. It would be twelve months before Joe found another job, and years before the industry completely recovered. My parents found themselves out of work shortly after us. It was the first time in my adult life that I faced such an unfamiliar and scary thing—we would quickly be out of money and jobs were scarce. I had two babies still in diapers. It was time to get resourceful.

Mom and I began to hand-dye silk and sell it on eBay® to make some extra money. We were soon doing very well with it and selling as much as we could produce. It took our minds off greater issues and helped with some of the most basic expenses at home.

We needed to do something bigger if we were going to recover. So when the family gathered at Thanksgiving, I rolled out a plan I had hatched in the wee hours of the night. I had begun to write a book all about different types of wool for hand spinners. With the help of the family and a loan from Dad, we could self-publish the book and sell it via the internet. There was more... while researching the wools and different fiber, I had connected with a person who led me to a new fiber to share in my book... made from soy. I wasn't exactly sure what to do with the soy fiber then, but I knew it had huge potential.

You could hear a pin drop at dinner when I rambled on about selling books with wool in them and this new fiber that no one had heard of made from soy. Everyone looks back on that moment and laughs now, but to their credit, they listened. I'm not sure they completely understood or entirely believed in my idea, but they believed in me and unanimously offered up their support. My mother was my first and only investor. As she handed me the check to start this project, I told her that if I failed, I would probably never be able to repay the money. With a big hug, Mom whispered into my ear, "We can make this great!"

Rising from the Ashes

South West Trading Company started over dinner that night. From the dining room table to our small garage, the company grew and succeeded. Mom and I worked around the clock to produce and sell *The Spinner's Notebook*, which sold thousands of copies worldwide. We bought our first container of Soysilk® fiber and sold out of it in just weeks. We were the first in the world to introduce soy for knitting and spinning, pioneering earth-friendly hand knitting fibers. At the time, we didn't realize what an impact this would have on the industry and our lives. We started a trend that everyone else would soon follow.

Dad and Joe spent hours each day packing orders and standing in line at the post office. They worked behind the scenes whenever we needed them... then dusted us off and pushed us to keep going when we were too exhausted to persevere. Within six months, we had outgrown the garage and moved to our first warehouse.

Now, five years and two more warehouses later, South West Trading Company yarns and fibers are sold worldwide. My mother, father, and husband are employed full time at SWTC, joined by a talented team of people we have met along the way. This company is our pride and joy. We have learned from each other and from the many amazing professionals in the yarn industry who have welcomed us, mentored us, and supported us. It has been an incredible journey.

Our first yarn in Soysilk® fiber was named "*Phoenix*". Most people assumed it was named after the city in Arizona near us, but that is not the case. We named it *Phoenix* for the mythical bird that rises from the ashes, a reminder to us of our beginning and our inspiration.

Soysilk® fiber is made from the residue of soybeans used in tofu manufacturing. This process is natural and free of any petrochemicals, making it an extremely environmentally friendly product. Soy is a completely renewable resource, coming from the earth and being wholly biodegradable. As early as the 1940's, textile experts dreamed of a fiber made from soy. (In fact, Henry Ford had a suit made of soy as an early prototype.) Soysilk® fiber offers superior moisture absorption and ventilation properties along with beautiful draping, softness and warmth. Today, SWTC yarns from Soysilk® fiber include *Phoenix, Oasis, Karaoke, Pure, Inspiration* as well as *Rock* from the Vickie Howell Collection from SWTC.

In 2003, we were the first yarn company to introduce bamboo fiber yarns. Today, bamboo yarns continue to entice and excite.

SWTC bamboo yarns can be found under the brand names of *Bamboo*, *Twizé*, and *Love* from the Vickie Howell Collection... look for more in the future. We love bamboo. It is a strong fiber that is cool to the hand and very soft. It is known for bright, strong colors and well-defined stitches in a finished garment.

In 2006, we introduced corn yarn with the launch of *aMAIZing®*. We first came across corn fiber three years earlier as a fiber for hand spinning and we knew it was special. We were thrilled when we finally developed a yarn from corn that is machine washable and dryable. We love *aMAIZing®* for children's garments and clothes for ourselves — it's a super soft yarn that is machine washable and dryable, making it earth-friendly and practical. From the polylactic acid in the corn plant, this yarn brings another earth-friendly choice to our artistic palette. Corn is an annually renewable resource and no fossil fuels are used in the production of this wonderful fiber.

Perhaps our most exciting yarns are the 2007 collection. We were honored to team up with *Knitty Gritty* star Vickie Howell, who created a collection of extraordinary yarns with us. The world was quick to embrace *Craft*, combining Milk fiber and Organic cotton; *Rock*, showcasing Soysilk® fiber, hemp, and fine wool, and finally *Love*—the only possible word for Bamboo and Silk combined. Vickie's style and personality are reflected in every aspect of this collection, which is already receiving rave reviews.

Adding to the excitement SWTC presents its first sock yarn, *TOFUtsies*™ which debuts another new fiber made from shrimp and crab shells alongside *Inspiration*, a luxurious Soysilk® fiber and alpaca blend.

I wish Nona and Nonie had lived to see how popular knitting has become and to see their legacy—South West Trading Company. With little formal education, they were smart in ways only life teaches you. These dear ladies are and will always be our inspiration at SWTC.

There have been many times over these years that I have sat somewhere, quietly pondering a decision and wishing Nonie and Nona were here to guide me. Nona is the voice in my ear when I think about different designs, designing yarns, and teaching new fiber people about the art itself. Their message of simplicity has guided us and we know they would have been proud that we have kept our yarns natural and provide good value.

Abbreviations

Knit

CC – contrasting color

cn – cable needle

cont – continue

C2R – (cable 2 right) Knit 2nd stitch on left needle, then knit 1st stitch.

dbl inc – (double increase) Knit into row below, knit stitch on needle, knit into row below same stitch.

dec – decrease

dpns – double-pointed needles

inc – increase

k – knit

k2tog – Knit next 2 stitches together.

k3tog – Knit next 3 stitches together.

l inc – (left lifted increase) Knit into the back of the stitch in the row below stitch on needle.

MC – main color

M1 – (make 1) With tip of left needle, lift strand between last stitch knitted and next stitch from front to back. Knit the lifted loop through the back of the stitch.

p – purl

pat – pattern

p2tog – Purl next 2 stitches together.

pm – place marker

psso – pass slipped stitch over

rem – remain(ing)

r inc – (right lifted increase) Insert left needle tip into the back of the stitch below the stitch just knitted. Knit this stitch.

rnd – round

RS – right side

selv – Work selvedge stitch.

sl – Slip next stitch.

ssk – (slip, slip, knit) Slip next 2 stitches to right needle 1 at a time knitwise. Insert left needle from left to right through these stitches and knit together.

st(s) – stitch(es)

St st – Work in stockinette stitch (knit on RS, purl on WS).

WS – wrong side

YO – yarn over

Crochet

bs – (bullion stitch) Wrap yarn around hook 5 times, insert hook into stitch, wrap yarn around hook, insert hook into same stitch, wrap yarn around hook, draw through all loops on hook, ch1 to close st.

CC – contrasting color

ch – chain

cont – continue

bpdc – (back post double crochet) Place yarn over hook, insert hook from front to back between next 2 stitches, then bring it forward between the stitch being worked and the one after it. Complete the double crochet.

dc – double crochet

fpdc – (front post double crochet) Place yarn over hook, insert hook from back to front between next 2 stitches, then back again between the stitch being worked and the one after it. Complete the double crochet.

hdc – half double crochet

MC – main color

pat – pattern

rem – remain(ing)

rnd – round

rs – right side

rsc – reverse single crochet

sc – single crochet

shell – Work 2dc, ch1, 2dc in same stitch.

sk – skip

sl st – slip stitch

sp – space

st(s) – stitch(es)

trc – treble crochet

WS – wrong side

Disclaimer and Credits

The origin and design of some of the garments shown in the family pictures are original, some are not. Most of the patterns are long since lost. They are shown only as family pictures. The patterns in the book are all original patterns created and owned by SWTC Inc. They have been created by the following talented designers:

Cindy Carlson	Joan Somerville
Elizabeth Freeburg	Vivian Tng
Lorna Miser	Karola Wright
Amy Polcyn	Diane Zangl

It has been our honor and privilege to work with many of these ladies since we began SWTC Inc. Their creativity and talent bring our yarns to life. My heartfelt thanks goes out to these and all of the other talented designers who have shared this adventure with us.

This book was published as a cooperative venture between SWTC Inc. and our long-time collaborator Shannon Okey, best known for her Knitgrrl series and other knitting books, but also for teaching classes on alternative fibers. Shannon ordered Soysilk® fibers for spinning from us not long after SWTC opened its doors! She later founded her own publishing company, anezka media, to bring exciting new books about knitting and other crafts to market. We look forward to a long partnership with anezka media, and many more books about knitting that matters.

The incredible layout and graphic design was the work of our talented friend and collaborator, Big Al Gruswitz of Boundless Creativity. His style and talent have advanced the marketing approach and graphics of SWTC giving us a world-class image. Al brought my words to life in this book with his creative vision and artistry.

Special Thanks to Amy Polcyn for proofreading this book. Amy is a true friend to help us out with this project and assure that our beautiful book was perfect!

—*Jonelle*

For more information on Big Al Gruswitz and Boundless Creativity please visit www.boundless-creativity.com and www.portfolios.com/profile.html?MyUrl=AlGruswitz

For more information on Shannon Okey and anezka media please visit anezkamedia.com or knitgrrl.com